The Storyteller

Retelling the Parables of Jesus.
My Journey in God's Love and Grace.

David Collins

The Storyteller: Retelling the Parables of Jesus.
My Journey in God's Love and Grace.
Copyright © 2021 David Collins
Publisher: Little King Books,
203/220 Tristram Street, Hamilton, New Zealand 3204

Bible translation permissions:

Unless otherwise noted, scripture quotations are from the New Revised Standard Version Bible, copyright 1989, Division of Christian Education of the National Council of the Churches of Christ in the United States of America. Used by permission. All rights reserved worldwide.

KJV: The King James Version (Authorised): Public Domain.

NLT: The Holy Bible, New Living Translation, copyright © 1996, 2004, 2007 by Tyndale House Foundation. UBP of Tyndale House Publishers, Inc., Carol Stream, Illinois 60188. All rights reserved.

NIV: 'The Holy Bible, New International Version', NIV® Copyright © 1973,1978, 1984, 2011 by Biblica, Inc. Used by permission. All rights reserved worldwide.

GNB: Good News Bible © 1994 published by the Bible Societies/HarperCollins Publishers Ltd UK, Good News Bible© American Bible Society 1966, 1971, 1976, 1992. Used with permission.

JUB: Jubilee Bible (or Biblia del Jubileo), copyright © 2000, 2001, 2010, 2013 by Life Sentence Publishing, Inc. Used by permission of Life Sentence Publishing, Inc., Abbotsford, Wisconsin. All rights reserved.

THE MESSAGE: Copyright © by Eugene H. Peterson 1993, 1994, 1995, 1996, 2000, 2001, 2002. Used by permission of Tyndale House Publishers, Inc.

MIRROR: The Mirror Copyright © 2012. Used by permission of The Author.

Cover Photo: Anestiev # 4975726 (www.https://pixabay.com)

ISBN 978-0-473-57766-7 (Softcover - POD Amazon)
ISBN 978-0-473-57767-4 (Kindle)

Dedicated to Jack and Brenda.
Parents who placed me in a world where
Christ was the obvious reality.

CONTENTS

1. The Sower 33
How a people who lived with a religion of walls and the fear of not measuring up, heard about a God of generous grace and love who never gives up on them.

2. The Weeds Among the Wheat 43
How Jesus encouraged his band of radiant followers, and warned those who sought to drag them back to the stifling requirements of law and ritual sacrifice.

3. The Mustard Seed and the Yeast 53
Two stories that tell us the world is getting better, not worse, that the peaceable kingdom is advancing, and that we can possess an optimistic and beautiful worldview.

4. The Lost Sheep, Lost Coin, and Prodigal Son 63
Three stories through which we learn that there is no part of the world, no matter how lost or godless, that has not been found by God in Jesus and reconciled to God.

Introduction

The Mooltan sailed into Port Otago in the deep south of New Zealand in 1849. It was Christmas Day. Her long, arduous passage from Scotland had been devastated by cholera and many hopeful of starting a new life in these far away islands died before ever setting foot on land.

Two months earlier the Mooltan was off the coast of Africa. Elizabeth Purdie feared that what she wrote would be barely legible because of the pitching of the vessel. But this would be no ordinary entry in her account of the passage. Elizabeth was 37 years of age and my great, great grandmother.

"Open your atlas, my dear young friend - turn to the map of Africa between 12 - 10 North latitude and 20 longitude. Midway abreast of the river Gambia and Rio Grande - then open your precious Bible. Rev 20 v.13 "And the sea gave up the dead which were in it". Our sweet Rose - I mean all that was mortal, slumbers neath those vast waters.

"On Thursday 4th October - in our little cabin - with all the children gathered around - with her head on my bosom - she gently drew her last breath. And yet we felt thankful that she died not of cholera - that she was not hurried immediately from any access, and bedding and all consigned to the deep. No we had a coffin made for her and the Captain very considerately said that if the doctor (Elizabeth's husband, William) would allow him, he would put the body into one of the side boats till night and when I was asleep he would see it buried."

William and Elizabeth would hardly have time to grieve, they had nine other children for whom they cared and then the good doctor was constantly attending to the sick and dying aboard the Mooltan.

Families were distraught, passengers and crew were fearful and emotions overflowed against the hapless ship's doctor. I don't know how you pick yourself up from such a devastating start, but William and Elizabeth did just that.

William was a storyteller, and as family legend tells, he would ride on horseback across the countryside of the Otago province: not only to bring medical care to his patients but also to tell the story of the great Storyteller - Jesus Christ.

1949-60 Wellington

I started hearing Jesus' stories before my school years. Born and living in Wellington, New Zealand. The second child of Jack and Brenda - devoted followers of Jesus Christ. They made sure I heard the Storyteller's stories. Much of that hearing was in the big old church where my grandfather played the huge pipe organ.

He did that for sixty seven years! His name was Charles. He made it into the Guinness Book of Records for such a feat! And the great Storyteller's name, his love and mercy, rang out through sixty seven years of grand hymn singing.

I was never a gifted storyteller. Shyness and timidity haunted me throughout my childhood. My earliest vivid memory is of my first day at kindergarten in Island Bay, Wellington. I still don't know how it happened, but as soon as this 3-4 year old boy realised his Mother had snuck away - I raced to the kindy gate in search of her, tears streaming down my face. Distraught.

A few years later in the Sunday School of that big old church, I was unexpectedly asked to sing a verse of a Christmas carol we were practicing - to sing it solo! A brighter red nor racing heartbeat had ever befallen a child. This carried on through my days at school. Don't ask me to say or sing or do anything before a group of any size. I was no storyteller.

1963 Huntly

During Easter 1963, the preacher at youth camp told the story of Jesus. I really wanted to walk to the front of the meeting to profess my faith in Christ as the preacher was urging his congregation of campers to do. But not this shy thirteen year old! No! I went the other way, out the rear door, back to my bunk room where, on the top bunk, I did what I knew I'd be doing had I walked forward with the others. All by myself, I surrendered my life to the loving forgiving God. All by myself, I felt an unusual peace fill and wrap around me.

By then we'd moved north from Wellington and I was attending Huntly College and the small Baptist Church not far from there, carefully avoiding any circumstances where I might stand out.

My Dad was a bank manager and had been posted to Huntly in New Zealand's Waikato province - a position he held for five years before moving to Auckland, our largest city. I completed my high school education in Auckland and then it was back to the Waikato; this time to Hamilton and the University of Waikato. Not possessing any notion of a future career path, I would commence degree study in the social sciences.

During my last year of high school, I had been chosen to spend two weeks at Outward Bound in the Marlborough Sounds. At 16, I was the youngest on the course, advertised as "Showing people their full potential through outdoor challenge and adventure". I loved and hated it for all the right reasons and grew in my estimation of what I could do. Sailing, kayaking, tramping, orienteering, survival and that 6.00am daily plunge into the chilly waters of Queen Charlotte Sound.

In some activities I bettered my older course cohorts; and by the time the course finished, was as fit and as confident as I'd ever felt. I eventually read the course master's assessment of my efforts. I've forgotten all of it, except one word - diffident. I looked it up:

"The adjective diffident describes someone who is shy and lacking in self-confidence. If you are shy and have a diffident manner, you should probably not choose one of these professions: substitute teacher, stand-up comic, or lion-tamer." (Vocabulary.com)

I would later become all three … allegorically speaking.

1968 Hamilton

It was Saturday night so I checked the cinema advertising section of the Waikato Times. I noticed a single column advertisement for

"Meetings with the power of God and divine healing" - at least that's the bit that stood out. So why would I be interested in that? I have no idea. It was language completely foreign to my limited experience of God kind of things - except perhaps from some of the stories of the Storyteller I'd heard or read.

What I didn't recall, or associate, was that just five days earlier I'd been at another Easter camp with combined youth groups. Something different was going on, or so my friends said. Ever compliant, I simply believed what they told me … some of the groups and their leaders … spoke with tongues!

I'd never heard of this before, but I took on the indignation of my friends and agreed that this was not proper. Apparently speaking in tongues led people into a lurking danger called … emotion; and we didn't welcome that, not in our church!

The final camp meeting was on Monday morning; and the speaker that morning was a youth leader - a youth leader who spoke with tongues and had emotion! But no one had told me, so I just thought his talk was … moving and challenging and passionate and really, really good. So good that when he invited young people to "stand up right where you are if you have never confessed that you have surrendered your heart to God" - I stood up!

Two hundred young people saw me.
But I meant it.
I really wanted to do it.
I tamed the lion and stood up.

Now, five days later, I'm in a meeting with people I'd never met before - not one of them. They were singing songs I'd never heard before. I think they had emotion. I think they spoke with tongues.

The weekend before I had agreed with my friends that I wouldn't have anything to do with people like this. They did things I'd never seen in church before. I went back the following night ... the lion tamer went back.

The small hall was packed and I found my place standing along the back wall - I was late, and the preacher was starting. He was a storyteller and tonight's story was about a lion tamer - sort of. A David who had protected his grazing sheep against a bear and a lion, and then his nation against a spear wielding giant. The preacher finished.

Some people had started going to the front as he spoke about different things for which he would pray. Then lifting his head he said, "And there's a young man standing at the back, who God is calling." Now there were several young men standing at the back, and I'm sure it applied to each of them. The only way I can explain this is to say that somehow, right at that moment, I heard that call internally as well as with my ears. I started walking.

For all my indecision concerning life after university, I was certain of at least one thing, I didn't want to be a minister. Now I'm walking to the front. Now I'm saying, I'll do anything for you, God. I'll be a minister. A storyteller. I'll stand out.

I was the first person I'd ever seen 'slain by the Spirit'. This terminology, I later learned, was used when a person is so deeply and powerfully touched and filled by God that they can't stand up. By the time I got back to my feet I could speak with tongues … and I had emotion! I felt different, I felt confident - empowered by the Holy Spirit.

I became a teller of the story of Jesus Christ. Just as so many of my forbears had been - whether on horseback, by music, through acts of service and love, by pen or by standing to speak. The honour of telling the great Storyteller's stories, and that of the great Storyteller himself, was now my simple passion. I was emotional!

Chronology Part One
(1969 to 2000)

1969-70 Apprenticeship

In the two years following my encounter with the Holy Spirit, I lived at home in Auckland. I grew in my call and passion in a small church where Pastor Shaun mentored me in the crafts of leadership, study of scripture, worship, expressions of the Holy Spirit and storytelling. It was like an apprenticeship. I formed many rich friendships. Many of these new friends were apprentices too.

During these years, our church was growing and purchased a large beachside rural property to develop as a camp and conference venue. Many well known international speakers would be hosted there during the annual Christmas Conference and the many events staged for pastors and leaders.

It was there that I heard the Canadian teacher Dr Ern Baxter. As I was listening, rapt at Dr Baxter's teaching, a seed of truth was sown in my heart that wouldn't come to life for another forty years. A seed that would help me comprehend the cosmic scale of Christ's work on the cross and shake off the limitation of thinking merely in individual, personal terms, about reconciliation to God.

1970-74 Marriage

In 1972, the church sent my friend Graham and I on a mission tour of Asia. We visited seven nations in East and South Asia, and made warm connections with Kiwi's who served and told the Jesus stories in those countries.

When departing for this trip, I met a girl at Auckland's airport. Suzanne's Mother was part of the group from our church who came to wish Graham and I well in our travels. Suzanne wasn't at the airport to meet me, because she lived nearby, she was there to see her Mother. But I fell in love.

When travelling in the dark of night by bus on Java's mountain roads, I asked God if I could meet Suzanne again. I asked the Almighty if I could marry her. Two years later, on 2nd November 1974, Suzanne and I married.

1975-81 Taupo

A month before we wed, our pastor told us he'd been contacted by the pastor of a church in Taupo (a tourist town on the edge of

New Zealand's largest lake). A few weeks after Suzanne and I had returned from our honeymoon, we moved to Taupo. We were the new pastors in the picturesque town. I was 24 years of age, my new bride - 21.

By the time we left Taupo seven years later, our portfolio of mistakes and successes, lessons and skills learned, laughter and tears, prized colleagues and good friends was full. We'd built a house and made a home for three beautiful children. We handed over the pastoral leadership of the church, sold everything, said tearful farewells and … headed for California.

1981-83 California

Toby was 5, Kent 3, and Terri 2 years of age. We landed at LAX with eight full suitcases. It was everything we owned. We were there for adventure. We were there to serve our old Kiwi pastor, Shaun Kearney, who with his family had moved to the United States with a dream to plant a church in North County San Diego.

Two years later we headed back to New Zealand with another portfolio full of experiences: from Mexico in the south to Alberta, Canada in the north and all the West Coast States that lay between. And, of course, stories to tell from the big wide, eye opening, startling world of Christianity USA.

1983-85 Whangarei

Youth with a Mission's Mercy Ship, the Anastasis, berthed at Port Whangarei in Northland, New Zealand. Aboard were the furnishings and belongings from our home in California. We had accepted the offer of a generous friend to serve with him in his vibrant church in Whangarei.

Our relationship was a reflection of the thinking we shared about the nature of the Church and the Kingdom of God. In those days, my belief that the Church in a nation was better served by relationships of brotherly love rather than hierarchies of rank and anointing (how God calls and gifts a person) was very important to me - and I am still decidedly of that view.

And in those days, a belief that entrance into the Kingdom was to be attained by the worthiness of a person's life was taught in the Whangarei church. I taught it myself.

(Note: we made a distinction between the Kingdom and eternal life. We saw the Kingdom as a realm of authority to be exercised on earth; but held that eternal life was a gift of grace attained, not by us, but for us by Jesus Christ).

However, the fruit of that particular view of 'entrance into the Kingdom' proved to be divisive, full of striving, and to some extent, elitist. Subsequent study and experiences with God have enabled me to dismiss this teaching.

1986-2002 Hamilton

Our family arrived in Hamilton in early 1986. We came with a church planting team of 6 adults and their children who had uprooted their lives because they believed in Suzanne and me and our call. We also came with the newest member of our family, Regan David Collins, born 16th April 1984.

Regan was adored by his older siblings, but all was not well with our youngest son. He suffered with eczema and not long after our arrival in Hamilton, we learned that Regan was asthmatic. The difficult daily care for our toddler placed challenging demands, particularly on Suzanne. Toby, Kent and Terri's days were filled with school, friends, sports and home life ... and loving their little brother.

South Pacific Fellowship.

The church flourished quickly but in 1986, cracks started to appear in our national relationships. The movement, through which we had formed bonds with other pastors and churches, shifted from being a relational fellowship that honoured the varying gifts among its members, to reform as a hierarchical body that elected Apostles to be over the churches.

Despite my advocacy for the status quo (and being called an "upstart little whippersnapper" for my efforts), the movement adopted this new corporate model. Twenty pastors with their churches broke away in order to retain the "relationships of brotherly love" simplicity that had served us so well. I was their facilitating pacesetter. We gave ourselves a name: South Pacific Fellowship.

The Hamilton church continued to grow: developing and making room for the gifts and passions of our members, sending mission teams to the Fiji Islands and ministering in nearby towns. We were telling the Storyteller's stories through many different media, in many different places. Family life was rich and full. We bought and sold a family home - and bought again, this time to add a second dwelling for Suzanne's parents to share life with us.

The Church at the Carlton.

In 1993 our church secured a lease on a downtown movie theatre. The Carlton had ceased operations as a cinema and we became known as the Church at the Carlton and continued to expand. Our worship and sound ministries loved their new venue and accomplished musicians and singers joined this happy band. Theatrical productions and a fabulous church choir were soon telling of the Storyteller's love and grace in their unique and moving ways.

And God moved … beautiful Holy Spirit moved in and it was encounter time. A remarkable season of refreshing as joy overflowed, love increased and unusual power touched people's lives. It was emotional and we were ecstatic.

Toby enthusiastically stepped up as our pastoral assistant. Kent had learned the drums and became a highly regarded part of the Carlton band. Terri had been gifted by angels with a voice to move hearts and a gift to lead choirs and congregations in worship. Regan made his musical debut in the Carlton's café, singing DC Talk's "Jesus Freak" as he worked his electric guitar.

Suzanne and I kept up a busy schedule telling of the Storyteller's life and retelling his stories at home, in churches and conferences around the country and during our much anticipated visits to Fiji.

Chronology Part Two
(2000 to 2017)

2000

On the 31st December 1999 we did what much of the world did as the Earth rotated on its axis with precision and over twenty four hours, ushered us into a new millennium ... we counted down the seconds with a crowd before the fireworks exploded above.

Toby had married Anna a month earlier. Kent and Terri were making plans to live in Sydney where she would study musical arts at Hillsong College and Kent would set up a flat for them, find work and help support his sister - Kent had always been the most kind-hearted brother and son. And so it was Regan, now 15, Suzanne and I who stood in the rain gazing skyward as the 21st century rolled in.

Regan had a small stature but a big heart. He insisted that we all should be loving one another. He'd battled with asthma for 15 years and those health contests had kept him … lean and lithe. To his bigger peers at school, in his rugby team or at church, he was the little guy they all looked after … and loved. Kent was twice his size (and seven years older) but Regan would fly into fun-fights with Kent … they were best brother buddies.

A phone call interrupted my quiet preparation on a sunny Wednesday afternoon in May. It was the Deputy Principal of Hillcrest High School.

"Mr Collins, Regan collapsed during his sports period and we've called the Ambulance; can you come to the school, please? I'll look out for you and direct you to where we've dropped the fence so you can drive directly onto the field."

As I drove onto the field I saw the ambulance. I saw the small huddle of people nearby and drove toward them.

I joined the circle of teachers and medics, Regan prostrate on the grass as the medics worked to maintain his pulse and his breathing - both were faint. I quickly identified myself and asked if I could say a prayer for my son. The medics respectfully made way as I knelt and took his head in my hands and prayed a prayer no one gets to rehearse. Some seconds later the medics resumed their work before placing Regan in the ambulance and suggesting I follow in my own vehicle to the hospital.

I called Suzanne as I drove - she was visiting a friend. As Regan was being connected to life support, I met Suzanne in the ward corridor.

Regan had not regained consciousness since collapsing on the field at the end of the class 12 minute run. Suzanne and I, Toby and Anna with two or three close friends kept vigil late into the night. I had phoned Kent and Terri a few hours earlier ... it felt like they were on the other side of the moon! The doctor explained to us the likelihood that a virus may have precipitated the cardiac arrest on the sports field.

We returned home in the wee small hours to see if it was possible to grab some sleep. We were back in the ICU with Regan by 4.00am. We joined Toby and Anna and our steadfast friends and resumed our loving affirmation of Regan, believing that he was hearing every word.

Regan died at 5.45am on Thursday 18th May. The line on the screen went flat - my son's line, the little guy, the one who insisted we should be loving one another.

I made the most excruciating phone call of my life. To Sydney, Australia.

Grief has the power to rob you of your greater story; but it can also become part of your greater story. For many months I didn't know which of these it would be, the questions and doubts came with force, the loneliness of grief stood in stark contrast to the sincerity and nearness of friends.

One day I read Psalm 116:15. I was quite familiar, I think, too familiar with the psalmist's words: "Precious in the sight of the Lord is the death of His saints" but that's not what I read. In the New Living Translation I read "The Lord's loved ones are precious to Him, it grieves Him when they die."

I stared at the page: I know what grief is, are you telling me you feel it, too? You also grieve for Regan? You weren't standing aside when grief crashed in, it crashed into you as well?

Eric Clapton was right. There are tears in heaven. I started to heal and grief became part of my greater story.

2003-06 Fiji Islands

Suzanne and I departed for the Fiji Islands in early 2003.

I'd been asked to provide consultancy services to the largest indigenous missionary movement in the South Pacific - Christian Mission Fellowship International (CMFI). Toby and Anna were the fantastic new pastors of our Hamilton Church.

I discovered that this "consultant" was also to be lecturer, mentor, budget advisor, conference speaker, fund-raiser, negotiator, project manager, mission team organiser and a fast learner of how to drive a four-wheel-drive Isuzu Bighorn though the deep mud tracks of the sugar cane fields. For the best part of four years we lived in Labasa on Vanua Levu, Fiji's large northern island.

By the time we had completed this most thrilling assignment, I had submitted several key reports to the President of CMFI and left behind a thriving training school - The World Harvest Institute. A school functioning with a confident staff, a mission-focused curriculum, a joint-relationship with Oral Robert's University and annual graduation ceremonies from which graduates emerge poised to go into the all the world as missionaries, church planters and pastors.

Those radiant storytellers can be found on every continent on planet Earth, apart from Antarctica!

2007-17 Auckland

Suzanne and I returned briefly to the United States in 2006. I never knew a 'Sabbatical' could be so much fun! We traversed the continent three times, visiting friends (and making new ones), churches and many of America's most famous cities and landmarks.

As we travelled we were completing Richard Foster's 'Celebrating the Disciplines' (based on his best selling book 'The Celebration of Discipline'). The practicums that accompanied the text stilled us, attuned us to the whispers of God and set us up to return to New Zealand with a confidence that we were in the very centre of his pleasure as we set off for our next adventure. Did we know what that was? Not a clue!

After itinerating through New Zealand, we received a call to take up the position of Senior Pastor of an Auckland Church. We accepted. It was our next adventure.

I resigned five months later. No, I'm not telling: except that it wasn't pretty, my doctor treated me for anxiety and depression and the church trustees made me sign a non-disclosure agreement.

A large group of people left the church at the same time. Some said to me, "We only stayed because we heard you were coming but now that you're going, we're coming too." We hung out together like a family of spiritual refugees. Eventually we called ourselves a Church and took on the name "Elevate".

The Shack

Wm. Paul Young wrote a book and called it 'The Shack'. During the first year of our infant church more than one person recommended that I read it. I held out for some time, then relented. I started reading The Shack. I mean, I couldn't put it down.

You know the story, don't you?

When Mack stood on the porch of the Shack ready to beat on the door to demand answers from Papa about the tragic death of his daughter - I was standing there with him (we both had a "great sadness" in our lives). And when the door flew open and seconds later Mack found himself in a warm embrace that started an avalanche of healing, of learning, of rising, of freeing, of grace and love ... it started for me a visitation, an encounter with the love of God that transformed me - that changed everything.

We led Elevate for ten years. It was the church that was unlike any I had been part of before. It was the church a pastor leads whilst he's having a visitation of the love of God.

I'd become a pilgrim.

> "A pilgrim is a traveller who is on a journey to a holy place. Typically, this is a journey on foot to some place of special significance to the adherent of a particular religion. In the spiritual literature of Christianity, the concept of pilgrim and pilgrimage may refer to the experience of life in the world or to the inner path of the spiritual aspirant to a state of beatitude." (Wikipedia - edited)

Mine is a spiritual journey. The very idea shocks the old me - certainty rather than curiosity was the value by which I lived. But I learned that someone who journeys often does so because they're curious at what lies just over the horizon and sets sail to find out.

Toby was a priceless help to me during these early days of visitation. His curiosity had started much sooner than my own and he was able to introduce me to theologians, pastors and mystics who would feed my new found passions. I would have the great privilege of meeting many of them, hosting them in our country and in doing so discovered an ever swelling company of like hearts and minds - New Zealanders who just wanted to journey.

Suzanne and I retired from pastoral ministry in 2017 ... storytellers who can't possibly be quiet.

In these pages I retell some of the great Storyteller's most compelling stories. We know them as 'The Parables of Jesus' and I was told them, and had them explained, numerous times from my earliest days. However, my experience in the love of God gave me a 'new lens' - the same wonderful stories read through healed, renewed and recaptivated eyes.

Chapter One
The Sower

Matthew 13:1-9, 18-2

One sunny day a happy sower went out to toss seed over his vast field. This was no ordinary sower - it was the King of love, the Father of all mankind, the delightfully happy God.

And it was no ordinary seed, the label on the sack read: The word of the kingdom - sow liberally for a bumper crop of goodness, peace and joy in the Spirit.

And it was no ordinary field, in fact it was the entire world of men and women, boys and girls - every beautiful soul who had ever been born.

So excited he was for his field that the happy sower tossed the seed absolutely everywhere - recklessly spreading it without thought of waste, making sure that there was not one patch of his field not generously covered with the life-giving seed. He wasn't waiting for the ground to first ask and there was not a soul left untouched by the goodness embedded in each kernel.

But alas, some dear souls had been trodden down and walked all over for so long that the seed went no further than to sit on the surface. Once carefree precious children but through many blows in life had become hard and suspicious that anyone would want to do them good or show them a sincere affection - it was like birds could just fly in and snatch the seed away.

Alongside all the rich malleable soil, were pockets that had never been broken - these dear people thought that to be vulnerable was to be weak, and a layer of resistance had formed just below the surface like a rocky substructure.

When first touched by the happy sower's word of peace and joy they rejoiced but then quickly hardened up so as not to be thought ill of or be troubled by their fellow invulnerables. The seed just never took root.

The sower's seed would bring about freedom - the anxieties associated with trying to become wealthy or important in the eyes of others would soon be dissolved and springing up instead would be contentment, rich relationships and a full life without the stress. However, those anxieties lurked like weeds in a few places and pounced on the seedlings of peace and freedom and strangled the very life from them.

Nevertheless the sower, ever hopeful and merciful toward his whole field, would not give up on those parts that had at first been unable to embrace and enjoy his seed-word of goodness and joy. Love never gives up.

The anticipation was palpable; the happy laughter could barely be suppressed as the King of love returned to view his field. No longer wearing the clothes of seed time, he's here to see the fruit of kindness, assurance and liberty now flourishing in the field.

There it stood - every plant showing off its delicious fruit. Some bore more than others, but to the Father of all, this was never a competition and he wanted to skip and dance everywhere, for this was no ordinary sower, this was no ordinary seed and this was no ordinary field.

"The mystics always seem to move in the direction of
a more generous inclusion, a deeper appreciation for mystery,
and the primacy of love."

Brian Zahnd

There was a time in my life when the big thing about the parable of the sower was its portrayal of those who didn't make it, who didn't cut it, who didn't measure up. But something profound had happened to me and the story just couldn't stay like that.

My world had been one of categories, of "them and us" thinking, of inclusion for some but exclusion for others - most others. There was only one category that was fully pleasing to God and that was those who managed, by no small amount of effort, to avoid the dis-grace of being like the metaphorical well trodden path, rocky ground or weed strewn field. Then having qualified for the description "good ground", made sure they were nowhere other than in the company of the "one hundred percenters".

It was exhausting! How many others had I ushered into such a place of striving, self-doubt and God-doubt by telling such a story?

When God in Jesus Christ turns up on the planet he soon finds himself in a city of walls. Jerusalem itself was a walled city; but then once inside there were a myriad of walls, gates and veils, defining the no-go zones for Gentiles, women, non-Levites and the unqualified to serve. Just like all my Parable of the Sower categories and boxes.

The supreme no-go zone was the Holy of Holies in the Temple. A massive heavy curtain kept everyone but an especially chosen few out. If that place could be breached, if that veil could be torn apart, then no other exclusive place would be safe from the broken, unqualified hordes. (You know the story don't you … it was shredded!)

When I experienced the love of God, it changed my picture of God. Paul Young had helped enormously, of course, by casting Papa as an African-American woman. Papa was the name for God the Father in The Shack. Do I think the Abba of Jesus is an African-American woman? Do I think the Abba of Jesus is a white-skinned male with masculine attributes? Those questions both are the point and miss the point! My God-image was inadequate: I'd never questioned it since a child - and the confrontation of Paul Young's Papa was just the shake-up I needed.

Periodically during those months of visitation I would tremble in awe and amazement - this was not a visible, external movement, but an inner excitement that I could feel. I think of John Wesley who spoke of feeling "strangely warmed" as he encountered God during his time with the Moravian missionaries. God was shaking me up in a good way as his love was bursting within.

With every shaking my vision of God-is-love would widen, another wall of exclusion would crumble and I would "move in the direction of a more generous inclusion." I was sailing toward a new horizon.

Papa was becoming the "happy sower (who) tossed the seed absolutely everywhere - recklessly spreading it without thought of waste, making sure that there was not one patch of his field not generously covered … not waiting for the ground to first ask … there was not a soul left untouched by the goodness embedded in each kernel."

After reading The Shack, I began to read C. Baxter Kruger's short book "God Is For Us". I have my son, Toby, to thank for introducing me to this delightful theologian. I've devoured every one of his books since and had the privilege of spending quality time with him during his visits to New Zealand.

The excited shaking returned - and I was barely a few pages into "God is For Us"! Baxter was writing about the enormity of the grace of God when he co-joined himself to the human race - all of us - in the Son, Jesus. The implications of being "in Christ" or "together with him" were mind blowing - as astonishing as perhaps they were to Paul from Tarsus when he exclaimed "Blessed be the God and Father of our Lord Jesus Christ who has blessed us in Christ with every spiritual blessing in the heavenly places" (Ephesians 1:3).

Christ Jesus vicariously represented every single human being; carrying every one of us as the heavenly places opened to him at his glorious ascension; when he sat down alongside the loving Father.

> "Paul is talking about being ushered into a fellowship with God that is so close, so intimate, so deep, so real, so alive that everything God the Father is, everything He has, all His treasures and glory are shared with us

personally." (Page 6. Kruger, C. Baxter. God Is For Us. Perichoresis Press)

If that was stunning good news, there was something else that's been life-changing.

"But we have not yet come to the full glory of the gospel. For it is not eternity, but history, that has set the apostle ablaze" (P.12) Baxter writes.

I stared again at the scripture, he's right! I exclaimed ... it's past tense! Paul is writing of that which has already been done, not of something that will happen at some future time when we pray the right prayer or make some move to get closer to God. We were included with and in Jesus 2000 years ago, before anyone knew how we would turn out! It's history!

My heart was being captured by the indiscriminate wonder of the love and grace of God. As recklessly as the great Storyteller had his sower toss his seed absolutely everywhere, I was starting to see that the gospel, that our good news is utterly good. There is no threat in it, no coercion, no demand - all is of grace and grace has been scattered on all! O what a story! O what a Storyteller!

"The gospel is not the news that you can receive Jesus into your life; the gospel is the news that the Father's Son has come and he has received us into his life", Baxter would later tell me.

When the story of the sower was first taught to me there was no redemption for the sorry ground that had been pounded under untold feet, had a resistant layer of rock somewhere beneath the surface or had menacing weeds hiding within. Why hadn't I realised the whole life of Jesus was a story where those whom everyone else had given up on - he restored, he healed, he gave life and dignity to?

Love ... Never ... Gives ... Up!

I had to feel it to know it - the old dogma of 'them and us', of 'in and out', was just too strong. But O happy day when I stood on the porch with Mack.

A Mystic

According to the much loved Franciscan Priest, Richard Rohr, many Christians are scared of the word mysticism ... but a mystic is simply one who has moved from mere belief or belonging systems to actual inner experience of God.

I realised I was a mystic! My inner experience with God meant something to me - it transformed me and it sent me to the beautiful scripture to see if anyone there was trembling in wonder at the Love they'd encountered - pretty much everyone!

A Generous Inclusion

I realised I was a grace guy! How on earth did unconditional, unearned, extravagant, over-the-top, excessively generous and including grace become so frowned upon? I needed all of that, as did the Sower's entire field.

Primacy of Love

And I realised I'd been ruined by love. That love is not just the main thing, it is the only word given to tell us about the very essence of God. I came to learn that for God to be love meant that there has never been a time when God was alone, rather God is a circle of love that flows in the eternal Trinity of Father, Son and Spirit ... and out into every created thing.

Meeting the Trinity in the kitchen of a shack where affection and laughter flowed as freely and as naturally as in any happy family (Chapter 7 The Shack). Feeling the welcome - that I was by no means intruding on something too holy for me; that they were ... my family. This was a gift to the deepest parts of me, a knowing that I truly belonged, that the acceptance and affection I saw there was as much for me as for any of them.

Knowing that Love is patient and kind (and the rest of 1 Corinthians 13:4-5), how could I think any longer that the Sower would first check their 'key performance indicators' before allowing himself to skip and dance with every part of his field ... his world ... his creation?

The wind now filling my sails - the journey was exhilarating!

Selah
Pause | Consider | Apply

During a reading of Psalms (songs) the word Selah is included in the text to ask the singer to pause - a brief interlude to ponder the composition is being called for. Following each chapter of The Storyteller, you will find an invitation to "pause, consider and apply" - to personalise what you have just read by completing three intentionally open sentences. Alternatively, the Selah interlude can be used to trigger discussion and testimony in a group.

The Sower

My picture of God has been formed by …

The words that describe the God I have experienced are …

My experience of God has resulted in me seeing people …

Chapter Two
The Weeds among
the Wheat

Matthew 13:24-30; 36-43

It was so satisfying - the end of a long day's labour. The whole field had been sown with good seed and the happy and contented farmer soon fell soundly asleep. His dreams would be of a field full of golden wheat swaying in the breeze in the days to come and a celebration of all he had worked for.

However this was no ordinary farmer, this was the King of love, the Father of all mankind, the delightfully happy God. And it was no ordinary field, it was the world in which men and women, boys and girls went about their daily lives.

The seed that the King of love sowed was also no ordinary seed; each seed was a person who had come alive with the good news of the gospel and were living as one's in whom the King himself had taken up residence - they were radiant children of Christ's Kingdom.

But overnight, an imposter turned up with a bag of different seed. It looked similar to the seed sown through the day but it was little more than a poor mutation of the real thing: if the first was wheat, then this was just a bag of weeds. Malevolently, he scattered his seed across the field.

This evil imposter aimed to ruin the whole crop and dash the dreams of the good farmer. He thought of the seeds he sowed that night as his children - they despised the freedom of the King's radiant ones and would choke them out if they had half a chance.

It wasn't obvious right away but, as the seeds sprouted and pushed their first shoots through the soil, it became clear that weeds were growing among the wheat. The wise farmer told his helpers to let them grow side by side, to pull on the weeds now would certainly damage the young blades of wheat - but leave them until harvest time, then harvest them both, separate them, bind the weeds into bundles and burn them - then gather the wheat up for himself.

And that's exactly what happened. The farmer's dream came to pass and the evil imposter was thwarted. What happened to the King's radiant children? Well they were more radiant than ever - shining like the sun by which the beauty of God's goodness could be seen by all.

"Lord, please restore to us the comfort of merit and
demerit. Show us that there is at least something we can do.
Tell us that at the end of the day there will at least be one redeeming
card of our very own. Lord, if it is not too much to ask, send us to bed with
a few shreds of self-respect upon which we can congratulate ourselves.
But whatever you do, do not preach grace. Give us something to do,
anything; but spare us the indignity of this indiscriminate acceptance."

Robert Farrar Capon

It didn't happen right away but the more Suzanne and I journeyed on in this more generous grace, the more like-hearted friends we made and the more some old friends decided to keep their distance.

But our experience was far less dramatic than that of the people who first heard the Storyteller tell this story. The keepers of religious law had much to lose and they reacted with envy and malice. They had enough trouble on their hands when Israel's latest prophet bypassed their splendid Temple and set up shop in the wilderness, by the river Jordan. It was more than insulting: people - their people - flocked to John to be baptised.

Now Jesus was choosing that wild place and that untameable prophet to inaugurate his ministry.

God skipped Church for one of his biggest days!

The Temple rulers and keepers of Israel's law were determined to stop this Jesus and his followers any way they could - and they kept up their malevolent scheme until the day they died. There was too much talk of love, too much talk of forgiveness, too much talk of grace ... besides, their sacred history, respectability and livelihoods were at stake.

We were only a few years into our journey, marvelling at the freedom of our personal spiritual renewal and someone coined the word "Hypergrace" - and made it a bad word! Books and blogs, videos and podcasts joined the charge - media unknown to the first opponents of abounding grace. What impact did this make on us? Nada! Not the tiniest bit ... El-Zippo! By the time someone got 'round to crying "hypergrace" we were too far gone in this indiscriminate acceptance and our life inside the Trinity, inside the heavenly circle of affection, was just too good, just too full.

The First Audience

The parable of the weeds among the wheat was first told to the people who would see it played out in their lifetime - the young Church of the first century - the first audience. It was an encouragement, a warning and a plea.

It was an encouragement to the radiant believers who had turned away from the stifling religion of the Old Covenant and the Jewish Temple, to find relationship with God through Jesus Christ - the unsurpassing gift of the grace of God. It was encouragement that no matter the trials and tribulation, despite the persecution against them, they would overcome to shine brightly in their Father's kingdom.

But it was a warning to those who would infiltrate the young Church with plans to haul them back to the requirements of law and ritual sacrifice. These Judaizers would perish in the fiery destruction brought by the Romans upon Jerusalem in AD70, just as the Storyteller had shown with those burning bundles of weeds.

The mention of the end of the age in this parable syncs with the same phrase at the commencement of Christ's Olivet discourse (the suite of warnings, prophecies and parables found in Matthew 24 & 25). It was the dramatic end [disappearance] of the Old Covenant or Temple age that Jesus would make obsolete in his death. (Hebrews 13:8)

Finally, it was a plea to everyone in the early Church not to heed the threats and machinations of the Temple. It was a plea echoed in the epistle to the Hebrews to not cast away their confidence in Christ, to not forsake the assembly of encouragement as some were doing and all the more so as they saw that day of destruction for the city they loved approaching. (Hebrews 10:23-25)

And Jesus' care went also to those who were in the most danger. Nicodemus was a Temple insider to whom Jesus appealed telling him that God loved all the world, impartially and passionately, and sent his Son to save them - those who placed their trust in Christ would not perish when the Temple came crashing down but would live ... forever! (John 3:16)

After the Storyteller had told the story of the Sower who had tossed his seed of goodness, peace and joy over absolutely every part of his field - a story dripping with extravagant grace - it made sense that his next story would show a firestorm of religious opposition from the purveyors of merit and demerit being unleashed.

The Storyteller knew that these zealots would be as infuriating to their Roman occupiers as they would be spiteful to his precious Church. He knew that their Temple would come crashing down in Rome's merciless revenge.

This was not God's judgment, it was Rome's. When we come to interpreting the metaphors of fire, loss and destruction, there is a powerful reality that forbids us from jumping to the conclusion that this is the judgment of God … God himself! His call to love our enemies and his pre-emptive strike of forgiveness (Luke 23:34). However, Rome's fury would indeed bring to an end the persecution perpetrated from the Temple against the young Church.

The Last Days

In 2014, Toby invited me to bring a teaching series in his Hamilton church. It represented an exciting shift in the story I had to tell about the future.

Before that time, before my encounter with God, the story I had to tell about the future was rooted in "futurism" (an apocalyptic interpretation of many major portions of the Bible - E.g. the Book of Daniel, Matthew 24, the Book of Revelation - as future). There was plenty to be nervous about ahead, not least, the possibility of being left out of God's promises to those who are living victorious lives.

The story I had once told kept my hearers working hard to ensure they would measure up, be worthy, merit the best God had planned for the future ... so that they could go to bed with a few shreds of self-respect and spiritual achievements upon which to congratulate themselves.

Both Toby and I now realised how much sense it made when these scriptures were viewed as history - events relative to the first audience of the great Storyteller. "This generation will not pass away until all these things have taken place", Jesus assured his audience who had asked about the end of the age (Matthew 24:34). The proverbial 'last days' were in fact the last days of the Old Covenant of merit and demerit.

Consistent with so many of the Storyteller's stories, this narrative was about ensuring the fledgling Church, who had been born in the abundant grace of the Father, would remain pure, without a mixture of law and grace and free from the marauding hostility of the Temple crowd.

With appropriate irreverence, I called the teaching series: 'The End is ... Fun!'

What an utterly freeing and thoroughly optimistic story I now had to tell. The good news had become gooder! Just like the Storyteller's metaphorical wheat - I started to see the shackles of requirement and measuring up fall off my friends who were embracing this story of God's extravagantly generous grace. I saw them, I saw myself, becoming more radiant than ever - shining like the sun by which the beauty of God's goodness could be seen by all.

Reading The Parables

The first secret to reading Jesus' parables is to know that God is love, that mercy, goodness and loving kindness are the very essence of the Trinity. It's to know that God's Kingdom is beautiful - it's the realm both inside and about us in which peace, joy and all that is good dwells in abundance through the Holy Spirit.

The Second secret to reading Jesus' parables is to know that they are primarily told to assure his first audience that God is completely for them, that he will warn them of coming trouble and save them from those who want only to enslave them. We too can take the same assurance.

The Third, is to realise the Parables are not detailed accounts of history or of things to come. They are allegories and their metaphors are broad brush strokes, not fine details. The audience is asked not to believe the metaphors but the fuller, hidden story they convey. Allegory and the use of metaphors places a limitation on how we interpret them and knowing the history of the first hearers really helps.

Selah
Pause | Consider | Apply

During a reading of Psalms (songs) the word Selah is included in the text to ask the singer to pause - a brief interlude to ponder the composition is being called for. Following each chapter of The Storyteller, you will find an invitation to "pause, consider and apply" - to personalise what you have just read by completing three intentionally open sentences. Alternatively, the Selah interlude can be used to trigger discussion and testimony in a group.

The Weeds among the Wheat

The unsurpassing grace of God toward me means ...

The biggest danger to living with the knowledge that God's grace toward me is unconditional and complete is ...

I am not fearful but optimistic about the future because ...

Chapter Three
The Mustard Seed
and The Yeast

Matthew 13:31-33

In the garden, just outside the house, a tiny seed was pushed into the ground with all the hopes that something wonderful would come from it.

Nearby, a happy cook could be seen through the kitchen windows, elbow deep in flour, singing as she took a measure of foaming yeast and poured it into the well she had made in the large hill of flour that was piled on the kitchen bench before her.

The gardener knew what he had planted would stay neither small nor hidden but would soon burst through the soil and grow and grow and keep on growing. Likewise, the cook knew that the measure of yeast that she had worked into the hill of flour to form a large lump of dough would permeate the entire lump and it too would swell and increase on its way to being the day's delight for the whole family.

But this was no ordinary seed, nor was the yeast just everyday yeast. No! They were the divine life of a loving King, they were the realm of this King's loving kindness and creative genius. When these stories were first told, the tiny seed and the measure of yeast were simply called, the Kingdom of heaven.

Oh, and if we have seed from heaven and correspondingly heavenly yeast, then we have just met the heavenly gardener and heaven's happy cook! Yes, the King of love himself, has done something that defies description for its splendour, something for the ordinary world of cooks and gardeners, mothers and children, the busy and the lonely … well, all of us regardless of race and creed. The world!

Later that day in the kitchen, a woman bent over to retrieve her newest creation from the oven. Squisito! the cook exclaimed in her best Italian - and indeed she and her family would find that there was no part of the loaf, not a mouthful, that wasn't completely delicious. Not one part that the yeast of heaven had not entered and permeated with its goodness. 'Divine!' She exclaimed again.

It took much longer, of course, for the gardener to see the full fruit of his labours - of the tiny seed he had long before pushed into the earth. Through the passage of time the young seedling had just kept growing, advancing, filling the space around it. Its progress had been relentless, unstoppable and, can I say, glorious!

The birds of the air had been watching what was going on. The magnificent tree that now stood where the seed long ago had been planted looked like home to them. They saw its strength as safety, its huge branches as the widest of welcomes. So they came from everywhere, a multitude it seemed, and made their nests there.

"The God of all is good, therefore he is
the lover of the human race."

Athanasius of Alexandria

There's so much to love about these two parables from the great Storyteller. For in these simple tales he makes it abundantly clear that this realm of his benevolent rule - his kingdom - has been progressively expanding, unhindered and uninterrupted, to infuse every part of society, every corner of the Earth, every endeavour and institution for the good of all mankind.

There's not a hint or word about evil in these stories. All we get here is the peaceable kingdom: the sun shining, the tree flourishing, the birds flying in and out as they raise their little ones who twitter away in their sheltered nests.

There are no elements of hostility or fear here. All we get is a happy cook working away with wholesome ingredients. An aroma filled house - freshly baked bread that sits on the table as chattering children take their portion and tell the stories of the day's adventures.

Following the turmoil in his story of the wheat and the weeds, the Storyteller is reassuring us that "all shall be well, all shall be well and all manner of things shall be well ... for there is a Force of love moving through the universe that holds us fast and will never let us go" (Lady Julian of Norwich, Revelations of Divine Love). The

Lover of the human race has set something in motion, and it is utterly good.

It's a Wonderful World

I first came across the idea of a world that is progressively getting better, not worse, when reading Kris Vallotton's book 'Heavy Rain'. In it he tells of a battle that erupted mid-flight when through his headphones Louis Armstrong's famous song, "It's a Wonderful World", was playing. The battle, of course, was in his mind as various verses from the Bible started warring against each other in a kind of battle for the truth.

The Lover of the human race was using Louis' song to, as Kris tells it, confront a "foreboding spirit" that "had lodged itself in my soul and was dictating my worldview." It was the beginning of a struggle that, by the time it had reached its conclusion, all the last days' doom and gloom lay defeated on the battleground of his mind, his spirit now freely singing along ... "And I think to myself, what a wonderful world."

This optimistic and beautiful worldview started to have a profound impact on how I saw people. Bible passage after Bible passage, author after author, were filling up my own soul with the truth that the God of all is good, that he is the Lover of the human race.

My own experience was starting to overflow to the people around me whom I had once so readily put into boxes and categorised as something other than wonderful and beautiful. It enabled me to engage with people with love and mercy (yes, we all need it). It taught me how to see the beauty of God in every soul and how eternally loved they were by their Papa.

Papamoa Beach

Whilst relaxing at beautiful Papamoa Beach, some Handel classics playing quietly on my iPhone, my mind upon the good news of God for the whole world, a girl of around 11 years old rode past on her scooter. As she did, she paused, turned, and with a broad smile said to me, "beautiful music" and rode on. It was a moment of true loveliness.

I recalled that there was a time when I would have believed a most dreadful thing - that upon reaching the 'age of accountability' (perhaps only a few years hence for this smiling happy girl); should she die an untimely death without ever personally receiving Jesus as her Saviour, she would suffer unthinkably in hell - in conscious torment, forever without any possibility of escape.

Such was the dogma I'd been taught and I had plenty of "soldiers" from the Bible to do battle for this idea. But I now had an experience, and an army standing up in the Scriptures that yelled NO!

It was so delightfully simple - and just like beautiful Holy Spirit to bring together a sunny day at the beach, G.F. Handel and a smiling girl to finally lay to rest the idea that the Lover of the human race could ever keep someone consciously alive in order to suffer such an unimaginably horrific eternity.

A quick study of the word "repent" reveals that it means to have a change of mind, to think differently. St Paul told the church in Rome that it was the goodness of God that leads us to repentance - to thinking differently. The opening lines of both John the Baptizer's and Jesus' public ministry were "Repent, for the kingdom of heaven has come near". They were telling us that now that the King of love's realm of goodness has come among us we're going to have to start thinking differently. At last I was!

After sixty years of life, thirty five of which had been as a storyteller - a pastor and missionary - I was at last thinking differently about God, about myself, about the human race, about the world, about the future and about ... hell!

Stops on Favour

This is what the Storyteller's mustard seed and yeast stories were saying to his audience that was locked into dualistic 'them and us' thinking (and 'us' were the good guys), an audience who had been told for generations about a God of punishment and retribution. The story of the heavenly gardener and heaven's happy cook would do battle against their worldview of exclusion and judgement. The Storyteller wanted them to think differently about the world, about God and the human race that he loved.

Only a few months earlier the Storyteller had been handed a scroll to read in the Synagogue at Nazareth, his home town. Rolling the two sides of the scroll he found the section from the prophet Isaiah and began to read ...

"The Spirit of the Lord is upon me, because he has
anointed me to bring good news to the poor.
He has sent me to proclaim release to the captives
and recovery of sight to the blind, to let the oppressed go free,
to proclaim the year of the Lord's favour."

(Luke 4:16-19)

He then rolled up the scroll and handed it back to the attendant and sat down.

A wave of realisation must have swept across the crowded Synagogue. Jesus had stopped too soon. Everyone had heard it so often it was the loudest silence when it didn't come, for following "to let the oppressed go free, to proclaim the year of the Lord's favour" Isaiah had written, "and the day of vengeance of our God." (Isaiah 61:2)

"Where's the vengeance part, Jesus?" they must have been asking. They were so accustomed to the idea of punishment and of imminent doom in their religion - of people getting what they deserve, of an eye for an eye, of judgement for wrong doing. But Jesus stopped on the word favour, rolled up the scroll, handed it back and sat down.

Jesus had just changed a story that ended with vengeance to be a story that ends with favour.

The idea that people most certainly will get what they deserve if they don't pray the right prayer or follow some other prescribed route, no longer held up for me, can no longer hold up in the light of grace, in the light of mercy, in the light of a Storyteller who stops on favour.

Love really does win. It's a wonderful world … O yeah.

Selah
Pause | Consider | Apply

During a reading of Psalms (songs) the word Selah is included in the text to ask the singer to pause - a brief interlude to ponder the composition is being called for. Following each chapter of The Storyteller, you will find an invitation to "pause, consider and apply" - to personalise what you have just read by completing three intentionally open sentences. Alternatively, the Selah interlude can be used to trigger discussion and testimony in a group.

The Mustard Seed and the Yeast

Accepting that God truly is the Lover of the human race has been ...

During my life I have been confronted to think differently about a worldview that ...

It really is a wonderful world, I can say that because ...

Chapter Four
The Lost Sheep, Lost Coin
and Prodigal Son

Luke 15

Out in the hills a diligent shepherd had counted the last of his sheep as they strolled into the pen where they will be safe during the night. "One has not come home" he said, "one is out there as the darkness falls." Every one of his sheep were known to him and immediately he threw on his warm cloak and headed out into the night to search.

Back in the nearby village, a woman removed her exquisite headwear adorned with silver coins, only to notice one of the coins was missing. Each was of very special value to her so without delay she lit her brightest lamp and began to sweep every part of the house.

Also that evening as the darkness fell, a farmer walked slowly home. Waiting at the crossroads, an hour's journey from his farm, had become a daily ritual, longing for the day when a distant figure on the road would be his youngest son returning from a far country. The way the young man had left had been hurtful and worrisome to this caring father. "One day", he told himself "I shall hold him again."

Later that night, sudden joy swept over the shepherd for he finally located his lost sheep - he was not willing that any should be lost and would have searched endlessly for it, but now, as he carried it gently across his shoulders, he knew that all were safely home. He calls together his friends and neighbours and the celebrations begin.

Over at the woman's house the rejoicing could be heard all the way down the street, for the silver coin had been found. The image it bore from the start had not changed and its original value had never diminished - even while it was lost - but was now restored to the place uniquely reserved for it among all her treasures.

The next day, the loving father stood at the crossroads watching a distant figure grow larger and larger, Almost before any features could be clearly seen, he knew it was his youngest son … returning … coming home. The father gathered up the skirt of his robe and started running as fast as his old legs would carry him - all the way to a long tearful embrace with his lost son.

Despite the way the son had thought of himself when eating slops intended for pigs - like the woman's coin, he had never ever lost his original value and his father's unconditional acceptance affirmed that. He placed a ring on his finger, shoes on his feet, a robe replaced his tattered rags and feasting was ordered in celebration of his son's return.

But his elder brother objected. He believed that everything he'd received from his father, he'd earned through his faithfulness to him - there were things he'd done to gain acceptance. He'd not been a prodigal, why all the celebrating! However, the father's acceptance and favour had never come with conditions: "Son", he said, "you are always with me, and everything I have is yours."

"[Man] can certainly flee from God (he does so),
but he cannot escape Him ... He may let go of God,
but God does not let go of him."

Karl Barth

As Suzanne and I journeyed together in this more generous inclusion, we started to see that a person's, that mankind's reconciliation to God had little to do with how we respond to him or pursue him, rather, it has everything to do with how the Divine has pursued us. It is all of grace. The most stunning thing to us was that in Christ, through his cross, he has already found us and reconciled us to himself.

We fell in love with St Paul's mind-blowing good news to the Corinthians:

"For God was in Christ, reconciling the world to himself, no longer counting people's sins against them. And he gave us this wonderful message of reconciliation." (2 Corinthians 5:19 NLT)

Run that past me again, Paul ... "God was in Christ" ... you mean he wasn't standing apart from Jesus when he died, forsaking him, striking him with punishment meant for us? The Father was in the Son, present with him on Calvary's tree?

Yes! Paul answers. The world was there too! Every man, woman, boy and girl who had ever been born - the whole cosmos!

Really, Paul, everyone?

It's as simple as it's profound - God was "reconciling the world to himself". The whole world met God in the cross. The Father was there in his Son who had already joined himself with the human race and placed them in his death - all of them - so that when He died, all died, we were all there! (2 Corinthians 5:14 ... "all" is translated from the Greek word 'pas' which means "all, any or every").

Whoa, that's huge! So how did the reconciliation take place, Paul?

That's simple too ... God forgave us. It's right there, I wrote that part there too: "no longer counting people's sins against them". I know this'll floor you but ... that's the world, the whole world, forgiven by God, reconciled to God; for you, David, that's two thousand years ago. Done!

But what do I get to do? What's my part, Paul?

Oh, I wrote that there, too ... go and tell people everywhere about what's happened ... "he gave us this wonderful message of reconciliation."

That's it? You're telling me there's nothing for us to do to be reconciled to God, it happened before we were born? Whoa! this is massive, a breathtakingly "wonderful message" ... how can we not tell everyone!

You're getting it now. We tell them so they can live the rest of their lives dancing, singing, blessing, laughing, giving, hugging, telling, loving, serving ... rather than anxiously striving to do something and getting others to do something, that God in Christ has already done. Finished!

Good news

When the great Storyteller told these stories of sheep, coins and prodigals, he was in the serious business of telling good news. That's what the word gospel means; it is literally good news.

Notice it's news. News is the reporting of what has already taken place - usually something that means things will now be different. It's not good advice, nor is it a good possibility (which is what the gospel has become to many a preacher), no! We don't buy a newspaper to read good advice or of a good possibility - we want to learn what's happened, what's been done, what are the things that have taken place that may impact me and others in significant ways.

And so the Storyteller tells the good news story of a sheep and of a coin who did nothing to make themselves found ... their reconciliation with the good shepherd and the caring woman required no effort on their part. All they did was ... get lost. We read these stories and realise that all the work of finding and restoring the lost falls upon God - not on us.

And on the strength of these two stories we should not presume that the third story was told to contradict the message of unsolicited grace they proclaim. So what are we to make of the parable of the prodigal?

What the Storyteller uniquely shows us here is the exhilarating experience of seeing and comprehending the generosity of the father's unconditional embrace - the robe, the ring, the shoes, the feast - and celebrating that there was nothing the prodigal could do or fail to do to lose his father's complete acceptance.

The Storyteller must have hoped everyone listening had heard that, and that it was sinking in. Listening intently were the Pharisees and the scribes of a religion that understood God as One well practiced at excluding the unqualified. Also standing there were a rabble of ordinary people curiously named "tax collectors and sinners" - they had been marvelling at these stories of grace, redemption and restoration that had come about through

the love of a searching shepherd unwilling for any to be left unfound and brought safely home ...

of a woman who would not rest until every missing piece was found and restored to its proper and unique place ...

and of the forgiving father who above all else wanted to show his sons that his tender care and abundant possessions were always theirs. Both the prodigal and the pious were embraced by his generous grace - "you are always with me and everything I have is yours." (Luke 15:31 NIV)

The Storyteller wanted to have them think differently about God and their inclusion in God's redeeming and restoring love. That's why we have the word "repent" in two of these stories - it means to have a change of mind. That's why all three parts of this story tell us of the out-and-out joy in heaven when a single lost one realises and believes how rich the heavenly Father's acceptance and favour has always been toward them.

O it's good news!

"In the body of Jesus Christ, God is united with humankind, all humanity is accepted by God, and the world is reconciled to God. In the body of Jesus Christ, God took on the sin of all the world and bore it. There is no part of the world, no matter how lost, no matter how godless, that has not been accepted by God in Jesus Christ and reconciled to God." (Dietrich Bonhoeffer)

I had one last question for Paul.

Excuse me, Paul, why then did Jesus have to die? I mean, couldn't God have just ... forgiven us anyway?

I'm glad you asked me that. I'll answer in three parts.

Firstly, God had so much more in mind than a forgiven fallen creation, he was at work on a brand new creation. You see, when Jesus died the old humanity died with him ... gone, the old passed away: Jesus was "the last Adam." When Jesus rose from the dead, the whole of humanity rose with him! By way of death and resurrection, we became what God had desired all along: just as he is, unpretended relational love.

Secondly, the cross announced how far the love of God would go - how vast a chasm it (he) would cross to save the world. The cross exposed the deepest depth to which a human could fall: to mercilessly, unjustly and brutally murder God. To utterly despise, discard and destroy Love himself. To extinguish the healer who had walked among them, the one who had given the dead back to grieving widows and parents, to snuff out the lover of the human race. Love would go all the way to reconcile the Romans and Jewish religious elite who had plotted and carried out the depraved execution of the Son.

"Father forgive them for they do not know what they are doing." (Luke 23:34). They never sought that forgiveness, they never repented or believed to secure it - the searching Shepherd crossed the deepest divide right to the very heart of darkness and found them. Yes! There is forgiveness and restoration for you and me, no matter how far we've fallen, no matter how deep our shame.

"There is no point at which the Shepherd who followed the lost sheep will ever stop following all of the damned. He will always seek the lost. He will always raise the dead ... Christ never gives up on anybody. Christ is not the enemy of the damned. He is the finder of the damned." (Robert Farrar Capon)

The third part of Paul's answer in our astonishing imagined conversation was incredible. I'd asked him why Jesus had to die ... we'll go to the next chapter to hear this one.

Selah
Pause | Consider | Apply

During a reading of Psalms (songs) the word Selah is included in the text to ask the singer to pause - a brief interlude to ponder the composition is being called for. Following each chapter of The Storyteller, you will find an invitation to "pause, consider and apply" - to personalise what you have just read by completing three intentionally open sentences. Alternatively, the Selah interlude can be used to trigger discussion and testimony in a group.

The Lost Sheep, The Lost Coin and the Prodigal Son

I am thankful for the unsolicited grace of God because …

Understanding that a person doesn't lose any of their original value to God causes me to …

"Everything I have is yours" means to me that …

Chapter Five
The Hidden Treasure

Matthew 13:44

Joy and excitement hardly describe how the man was feeling as he walked away from the real estate agency. In his hand was a deed of title. That day he had secured possession of a field his heart had been set upon owning for a very long time.

The sum he'd paid to close the deal was no paltry sum. Such was his desire to make the field his own that he'd sold absolutely everything! He knew something about that field that had made the price he paid completely worth it; he knew there was treasure there.

The man had discovered the treasure that was buried there and hid it again before going back to the city to sell up and buy the field. People had wondered why the man was so happy: wherever he went children and their parents would gravitate toward him - his joy was contagious.

Selling all he had was first humbling and then agonizing. However the thought of the treasure that was buried in that field, the joy just ahead, strengthened his resolve. He endured the pain and disregarded what others thought of his passion.

Before the day had ended, the field was his, the title deed was in his name and the treasure he would claim as his own.

It was a day no one would forget, for this was no ordinary man, this was none other than the King of love, the creator and sustainer of every person who had ever lived.

And this was no ordinary field, it was the entire race of humankind since the very first man had been created.

And the price he paid for the field was nothing less than his life …

> of his own free will he gave up all he had,
> and took the nature of a servant.
> He became like a human being
> and appeared in human likeness.
> He was humble and walked the path of obedience
> all the way to death
> his death on the cross.
>   (Philippians 2:7-8 GNB)

And the hidden treasure known to him? They were the dead: buried out of sight to the living, but known to the King of love for they had been created in his image, flowing from the other-centred love that defined the relationship he had with his Father in the Spirit.

There was precious Adam and beautiful Eve, there were the multitudes held like captives hoping a day would come when the locks and hinges would go flying as the doors were smashed open. Hoping they would be led out as the King's captives.

And it happened. Because the Divine King was fully human, he was subject to death - like the rest of Adam's race. Death was a doorway to the place of the departed, and now with the keys to death and hell (they came with the title deed), he descended to the realm of the dead. He had a message to proclaim, to preach in that place, that those who were there had not heard before - that they, along with the living and those yet to be born, were counted in Christ's reconciling death.

The love that radiated from the King illuminated the halls of Sheol and light touched every soul. One of them had once written …

> "Where can I flee from your presence?
> … If I make my bed in Sheol, you are there."
> Psalm 139:7-8

Before the day of his death, before this descending, the King had said, "Very truly, I tell you, the hour is coming, and is now here, when the dead will hear the voice of the Son of God, and those who hear will live." (John 5:25)

The King would be radiating his love and preaching God's grace, forgiveness and reconciliation for three days. And then, taking Adam and Eve by the hand, he who had descended started to rise ... an entourage too numerous to count were following. He rose, they rose and ascended far above all the heavens. (Ephesians 4:8-10)

The grave had been plundered, Sheol had been harvested ... and the man who had bought the field had all his treasure.

"He descended to the dead."

The Apostles Creed (390 AD)

I've been honest with you throughout this book so I'm not about to deviate from that now ... neither Suzanne nor I have ever heard of this particular rendition of the Parable of the Hidden Treasure before. It may be far from anything the great Storyteller was thinking. However, the truths that I've woven through this retelling of the story are to be found throughout the Scripture and are well represented in the literature and art of early Orthodoxy.

Holy Saturday was never part of our tradition. We did Good Friday and Resurrection Sunday, but for some reason or other, Saturday didn't make the cut in our tribe. (Perhaps, unlike our Orthodox fathers and mothers, we were just ill-prepared to consider anything that hinted at a person being able to respond to Christ after death).

Imagine how stunned we were when arriving in these unchartered waters and there this rich piece of our history and of the truth about Christ came into view.

I often characterise this spiritual journey as moving in the direction of a more generous inclusion - it only made sense that we would eventually learn about the rich tradition of Holy Saturday - it has 'generous inclusion' and 'extravagant grace' written all over it.

I bought a copy of Benjamin Myers' book 'The Apostles' Creed'. I'd been enjoying viewing this Australian theology professor on You

Tube and the book didn't disappoint. As he addressed the line in the Creed "He descended to the dead", Ben Myers shared:

"In Eastern Orthodox iconography a glorified Christ stands over the broken doors of hell. Beneath his feet, the chains and locks that have held the dead are all broken. The doors of hell have come unhinged. The grave has been emptied. An old man and an old woman are depicted on either side of Christ. They are Adam and Eve. Christ has seized them by the wrists and raised them up from the shadowy underworld."

Soon after, I obtained a copy of the Icon "Anastasis" - the very depiction Ben was describing. This dramatic painting from the 11th Century announces its amazing truth in our apartment ... I marvel at its message every day.

Commoners

Following our retirement from pastoral ministry in 2017, Suzanne and I moved from Auckland to live at Ruakaka Beach in Northland, New Zealand. We'd built a house and enjoyed two years there, welcoming a slower pace of life, making new friends and hosting old ones at our home in Surfside Lane.

In early 2019 we sold up and moved back to Hamilton. It had been 16 years since we'd left our family and friends there and headed for the Fiji Islands.

Toby and Anna and their five children, our daughter Terri with her husband Ub and their two sons, were living the busy lives of young families there in our country's fourth largest city. It was fabulous being in the same place as our seven grandchildren and their parents - it was just the best move for us.

Our grace journey with new friends, favourite authors and the always near blessed Trinity, had helped us think more widely and graciously about the Church and about diverse modes of worship and fellowship. So it was that soon after arriving in Hamilton, Suzanne and I started attending and enjoying the communion of believers at Commoners Church in Hamilton. Commoners offered a more contemplative and liturgical style of worship, and a warm relational atmosphere of shared church life. As a bonus, we were hearing points of theology that resonated with our now decade long pilgrimage.

On the 31st of October 2019, we did something we had never done before. We gathered with our new church for a simple midnight service that honoured the One who 'descended to the dead', the martyrs of the Church and loved ones who had died. It was All Hallows' Eve (sometimes called All Saints Eve - the day preceding All Saints Day) and this was a first ever for us. It was Halloween.

Who knew that this evening of costumes, pumpkins and trick or treats was rooted in such marvellous theology? All my life, every church I'd been part of had failed to capture the opportunity to talk victoriously about death and the dead with their kids. Why hadn't anyone told me that All Hallows Eve was a celebration of

Christ's descent to the realm of departed souls and that he was there to proclaim his good news. That he was there because, just as in the parable of the lost sheep, ninety nine aren't enough - he has to seek even the last lost one. No wonder it is called All Saints Day!

That evening, with our friends from Commoners Church, we celebrated that extraordinarily good news; and we honoured the martyred dead - countless men and women throughout history who were not afraid of death. Saints who, where others saw only darkness and despair, saw broken gates and new beginnings.

I'd learned from Ben Myers that the ancient Church was so steeped in the message of Christ's triumph over death that they would assemble for prayer in tombs. It was a practice in Roman civilisation to bury the dead miles away from their cities so that the living were not contaminated. But the Christian's erected their church buildings over the remains of the martyrs and housed the dead in their Cathedrals. They made it so obvious - death has no victory, death has no sting!

That evening at Commoners Church, Suzanne and I remembered and honoured our son Regan who at sixteen years of age had joined the dead. There was nothing ghoulish about our service that night. It was gratitude, it was remembrance, it was worship and it was quietly triumphant.

Finished

When Christ on the cross cried "It is finished!" and breathed his last ... "At that moment the curtain of the temple was torn in two, from top to bottom. The earth shook, and the rocks were split. The tombs also were opened, and many bodies of the saints who had fallen asleep were raised. After his resurrection they came out of the tombs and entered the holy city and appeared to many." (Matthew 27:50-53)

The fear of death … finished! The captive hold of death … finished! Death as the ultimate power in the world … finished! It has no victory, it has no sting! And I have another, my third powerful answer to the question of why Jesus died.

From the prophet Hosea in the Jubilee Bible, "O death, I will be thy end; O Sheol, I will be thy destruction." (Hosea 13:14 JUB) … and the man who sold everything to buy the field had his treasure.

Selah
Pause | Consider | Apply

During a reading of Psalms (songs) the word Selah is included in the text to ask the singer to pause - a brief interlude to ponder the composition is being called for. Following each chapter of The Storyteller, you will find an invitation to "pause, consider and apply" - to personalise what you have just read by completing three intentionally open sentences. Alternatively, the Selah interlude can be used to trigger discussion and testimony in a group.

The Hidden Treasure

Next Halloween, I think I will ...

This "hint" that the deceased might be able to respond to Christ after death is ...

The relentless pursuit of every lost-one by Christ is amazing and ...

Chapter Six
The Wicked Tenants

Matthew 21:33-41

The lush green rows of the vineyard were everything their owner had pictured in his dreams and this season the vines were heavy with bunches of ripened grapes. Soon the harvest would be trampled in the winepress and the year's vintage would be resting in large clay jars. The happy vineyard owner could now leave for a long planned trip abroad.

This wealthy man was known for his kindness and generosity so the new tenants on his property settled into their work on his behalf knowing how well they would be treated.

But the following year when the landowner sent servants to collect his produce, the tenants turned on them, breaking the terms of their tenancy. They beat one, killed another and stoned a third as he fled for his life.

However, it seemed the landowner's kindness and mercy knew no limits for he sent, this time, a larger team of servants to collect the waiting vintage - but they were treated in just the same brutal way.

Ever forgiving - and a last attempt to restore all the hopes he had at first held for his much loved vineyard, the kind landlord decided to send his son. Like his father, the son had great affection for the vineyard and had wept over what had happened, longing for it to be a place of peace and blessing for any who would enter its walls. He wept knowing the calamity that would come should the tenants persist in their defiance.

When the tenant vinedressers saw the son arrive, they rubbed their hands with glee. "This is the heir! Let's kill him and have it all for ourselves." They grabbed him, threw him out and killed him.

According to the tenancy covenant between the land owner and the vinedressers, both parties were bound to certain consequences if the agreement was broken. If the transgression was grave, then the penalties would be harsh - a capital offence would result in a capital punishment. Once breached, the march toward any consequences would be relentless. It was like a legal ticking time bomb. This was a law that had wrath!

So it was that the Storyteller stopped his narration, turned to his engrossed audience and asked, "When the owner of the vineyard comes, what will he do to those tenants?"

The audience that day were none other than the chief priests and elders of Israel - the Temple elite and custodians of Israel's covenant with God. They said to him, "He will put those wretches to a miserable death, and lease the vineyard to other tenants who will give him the produce at the harvest time."

It's as if they had signed their own death warrant, for
the vineyard was the nation of Israel;
the landowner was their God and heavenly King;
the murdered servants were the prophets sent by God to turn the heart of the nation back to him;
the produce sought by the King was a joyful, free and loving relationship flowing like wine with his people;
and the compassionate Son whom they murdered was the Lord Jesus Christ.

"On the third day the friends of Christ, coming at day-break to
the place, found the grave empty and the stone rolled away. In varying
ways they realised the new wonder; the world had died in the night.
What they were looking at was the first day of a new creation,
with a new heaven and a new earth; and in a semblance of a
gardener God walked again in the garden, not in the cool
of the evening, but in the dawn."

G.K. Chesterton

As the months and years of delightful journey passed we realised that we were becoming more centred on the cross - the death and resurrection of the murdered Son. Our gaze was repeatedly looking back, not forward - we were seeing that the most decisive moments in the great saga of humanity had already been enacted, that they were not waiting for some future time. It was the cross of Christ that was setting our hearts alight.

"As for me, God forbid that I should boast about anything
except the cross of our Lord Jesus Christ.
Because of that cross, my interest in this world died long ago and
the world's interest in me is also long dead."
(Galatians 6:14 NLT)

I was starting to disagree with the fifty year old me. Before my encounter with God, I believed that the most decisive events for mankind lay somewhere in the future. It was called revival, perhaps a mighty move of the Spirit. Without these, the salvation of the world could not be assured.

Instead of looking back and being able to rest in a finished work centred upon the cross of Christ, my friends and I were looking forward to events that prophetic people told us were very close. We seemed always to be on the verge of something great, something that would change everything! When it didn't come, did we give up hope? Not at all: we examined our methods, improved our preaching, learned how to do better altar calls, perfected our praise, adopted better prayer strategies and ran courses to make the coming revival actually … come.

In other words, we got back onto the mouse wheel. There would be no rest.

There was no such behaviour in the early church. To them the Messiah had come and everything predicted about Messiah's coming had been fulfilled.

Gabriel

The angel Gabriel's visits were 400 years apart. The first to tell Daniel when to expect the Messiah (it would be four centuries later) and about the things that Messiah would do - would finish. The second visit was to Mary and Joseph who would nurture and care for the Christ-child, the young Messiah, until he was revealed as the promised coming One. And what would Messiah do?

"finish transgression,
… put an end to sin,
… atone for wickedness,
… bring in everlasting righteousness,

... seal up vision and prophecy and
... anoint the Most Holy Place."

(Daniel 9:24 NIV)

It was so clear, Messiah would be bringing in a new reality.

Gabriel was telling Daniel of a time
when God would no longer count sin against us
when God would reconcile the world to himself
when people would be made righteousness
when every promise of God would be fulfilled
when the heavenly place of God's presence would be the place in
which mankind would be appointed, adopted and accepted.

(2 Corinthians 5:19 & 21 and Ephesians 1:3-6)

The business of the Temple in Jerusalem was to receive daily
offerings for sin - sin counted. Reconciliation was temporary.
Righteousness was fading. Promises were not fulfilled. The Most
Holy Place in their temple had been devoid of the Ark of God's
presence for centuries.

In simple but very loud words - Messiah was going to put the
Temple rulers, Scribes and Pharisees out of business!

The Temple Priests and Jewish zealots – in fact, religion in general –
wants to keep people believing there are still things they must do to
be rightly related to God ... keep them thinking there's still a higher
realm to attain or a greater intimacy with God for which to strive ...
keep them feeling they are never quite enough.

It was the oldest lie in the book. "Eat this Adam, and you'll be like God", said the serpent in Eden, "do something! and you'll be who you should be." Despite God having already said that these humans were created in the image of the Divine, they swallowed the lie that set humanity on a course of spiritual striving, believing they were inadequate and working in order to 'be' something they already were. The lie blinded them.

Living out of 'doing' instead of living out of 'being', this needing to achieve and acquire - even at the expense of others, would lead "Adam", this whole human race into restlessness, narcissism, conquest, violence and war.

Mankind became further away from who God is and their own true being. The religion of the Temple repeated the serpent's words, in kind, every day … there will be no rest.

They will never hear that they have come "to fullness" in Christ, in this Messiah (Colossians 2:10 NIV).

No wonder the tenants killed the Son. They killed the Messiah who would put them out of business and pull people off the mouse wheel.

Dr Ern Baxter

The seed that had sat undisturbed in me for forty years - sown whilst hearing the teaching of Dr Ern Baxter - was coming to life!

He insisted that Paul's crucified "old man" (from Romans 6) was corporate Adam - the human race, not the individual! That "the body of sin" was something we were in, not something that was in us. Adam was a many-membered body of all who had been born since Eden.

United with Christ in death, corporate Adam died, the world, humanity died ... to be raised in a new man, a "second man" - Christ! (1 Corinthians 15:45-49). There was a new creation. "For as all die in Adam, so all will be made alive in Christ." (1 Cor 15:22).

Jesus did not come to save us from an angry God, or from some fiery eternity, no! He'd come to save us from Adam, from the lie in Eden, from the religion of never being enough.

We were starting to see the new wonder ... seeing it by looking back at the cross. 'The world had died in the night. There was a new creation, with a new heaven and a new earth; and in a semblance of a gardener God walked again in the garden, not in the cool of the evening, but in the dawn.'

We are punished by our sin, not for our sins!

Even after the murder of the compassionate Son, the religious elite of Jerusalem continued to persecute and murder his Father's servants. Year after year of defiance against the kind and generous landowner, the consequences of their sin moving ever closer.

Twenty years after the Son's murder, the tyrant Nero ascends to the throne of the Roman Empire.

Fifteen years later, he sends troops into Israel to put down a Jewish revolt

In March AD70, the Romans set up ramparts, hemming in the wicked tenants on every side.

Within a few months the tear soaked fears of the loving Son played out.

Jerusalem was crushed.

They were punished by their sins.

Jesus finished the first telling of this parable by saying to the priests and elders of Israel, "it will be taken away from you, but the joyful, free and loving relationship that flows like wine - the King will enjoy … with … another people."

God's response to sin is to forgive it, to break the cycle of its devastation, not perpetrate the devastation. But what happens when sin is repeated time and time again, when the disobedience against all that is good just keeps going?

Not punishment from God but sin and broken law executes its cruel retribution on those who serve it (Romans 6:12-13 and 23). To compare this to continuing to drive one's car whilst all the warning lights are flashing is seriously inadequate - but helps us see the point. Jesus knew that Jerusalem would soon feel the consequences of its sin … and he wept.

Some from the young Church went back, but the vast majority had seen a truth that the sin-conscious Temple knew nothing about. They remained true to a new wonder … 'the world had died in the night, there was a new creation'.

Selah
Pause | Consider | Apply

During a reading of Psalms (songs) the word Selah is included in the text to ask the singer to pause - a brief interlude to ponder the composition is being called for. Following each chapter of The Storyteller, you will find an invitation to "pause, consider and apply" - to personalise what you have just read by completing three intentionally open sentences. Alternatively, the Selah interlude can be used to trigger discussion and testimony in a group.

The Wicked Tenants

I got off the mouse wheel when …

Resting in a "finished" work doesn't mean I don't …

I'm changing the way I see the world …

Intermission

"My Dad's a rebel."
The occasion was my seventieth birthday celebration; with those four words my son commenced his speech in honour of his father.

Fifty friends had gathered for the party; a cross section from the different towns and settings in which I had lived and worked over the years. Suzanne had asked what gift I would like from her for my birthday and the best thing in the world I could think of was an evening like this of "love and relationship" ... I had newly discovered it was the meaning of life (a discovery made far too late in my life, I know).

"My Dad's a rebel."

Toby had everyone's attention, especially my own! He proceeded to speak of a number of occasions in my past when I'd made decisions or set a course against the comfortable or accepted direction of some in my particular fellowship of colleagues. He knew these choices were not motivated by personal gain and he spoke of them, and this characteristic, with affection. I felt genuinely honoured. It was a memorable occasion.

My most recent act of rebellion had no intent or prior thought attached. God-is-love had smashed into my life without my seeking for him to do so, a glorious collision that spun me on my axis and sent me giddily on a journey away from (it seemed like) all the certainties I had about life and God and the world and people and myself. Dad, the rebel. Yet despite the undoing, I felt more secure than I think I'd ever been.

Love does that. It's the end of trying to be. It's the end of a self that pushes others away for some form of preservation. It's the end of judging the other to shore up one's own stocks. Dad, the very happy and especially relieved rebel.

> Love is patient and kind.
> Love is not jealous or boastful or proud or rude.
> It does not demand its own way.
> It is not irritable, and it keeps no record of being wronged.
> It does not rejoice about injustice but rejoices
> whenever the truth wins out.
> Love never gives up, never loses faith, is always hopeful,
> and endures through every circumstance.
> (1 Corinthians 13:4-7 NLT)

Just to believe that God keeps no record of wrongs rebelled against so much of how I had seen God and mankind - most of my personal evangelical theology was built around the idea that God indeed keeps records of our wrongs.

Love is the counter-intuitive way. Sometimes rebels get lucky and collide with it.

Many of the stories the great Storyteller told began with him saying, "the way the King rules is like this" (or, 'the Kingdom of God is like').

When his followers asked him why he told stories, he replied that they, his followers, already knew how the Kingdom worked - they knew the way this King ruled - he ruled by love, love was the secret of the kingdom. Once you have it, well this love just keeps increasing.

"I tell stories" the King told them, "because I want everyone to understand and become part of this love revolution, however, it seems some will just never understand." (Matthew 13:10-13 - author)

Life on earth - especially life in Empires and rigid religious institutions - knows only rulership by power, by coercion, by threat and by winning. The way the Storyteller-King ruled was impossible to comprehend. It looked more like powerlessness and losing.

Kind affection is a rebellion against the status of the powerful. It's why they murdered God. It's counter-intuitive … and it's the most liberating force in the universe!

Ken

I very much desired Ken to collide with the God of all goodness, as I had. He was dying with only a few weeks to live and he knew it. Ken had asked me to be the minister at his funeral - but there was a clause - he didn't want anything religious in the service.

This meant Ken was a kind person who loved people - a good man to whom the Storyteller's stories had not been passed down through his family tree. On more than one occasion, a teller of the gospel had behaved so hypocritically that Ken had understandably developed some defences against these storytellers.

Over the next few weeks I sat with Ken to listen to his stories. I knew that without some initiative from above, any attempt I made to manufacture a Divine collision would be unsuccessful. So I rebelled. I went against all the certainties that had once been my security.

At the time, there had been a mention in media of a dying man's unusual utterance to his family who had gathered around his bedside. It was a story that circulated only because he'd been a high profile inventor, businessman and influencer. It was told how when near death he'd awoken and described a bright beckoning light he felt he was moving toward - a beautiful radiance - a presence of love.

I shared the story with Ken. We then recalled other similar stories that we'd heard of strange things - near death experiences - but of which we had not taken too much notice. I said to Ken ... I asked Ken, should he experience something similar upon dying, should he see such a light or see or feel such a presence of love, would he go towards it, not away from it ... please Ken? Would he open his heart to such a warm encounter ... please?

Without hesitation Ken said 'yes'. It was just a simple 'yes' predicated on the possibility that there could be something, someone better than anything anyone had been able to show him. It was a 'yes' maybe of hope.

It wasn't the kind of 'yes' my evangelistic appeals had asked for or my 'sinners prayers' had mandated. I was rebelling in favour of Papa who I had encountered and experienced as unconditional love and mercy. I was rebelling in favour of the Christ who had descended and preached to the dead (Ephesians 4:8-10, 1 Peter 3:18-19). I was rebelling in favour of a love that is so pure that the heart can find no resistance to it ... and falls into Love's embrace.

"My Dad's a rebel"

I love the Church, yet in all my years of Church-life I had never felt any permission to ask questions. To ask a question was to question. For most of my years as a pastor, I continued the pattern and kept up the aura of certainty - a soft kind of intimidation to keep the questions at bay. I had never learned vulnerability and it didn't equate with reigning by winning.

It was to be a jewel in the crown of my encounter with Love - the freedom to participate in love, in vulnerability, intimacy and joy with others. The Storyteller's stories and the story of the great Storyteller himself became rich with new meaning ...

... not only did they point to a recklessly generous God - a Trinity of unfathomable grace and unstoppable love [this has motivated the first seven chapters of this book] ...

... they were also an invitation to participate in the affectionate flow of God, to imitate the Storyteller, to be a generous lover of all mankind [this is where the next few chapters of this book will head].

I had been trained to be less than generous, to keep the category lines clear - but those days were over, I'd been ruined by love. Besides, I was Dad, the rebel.

Chapter Seven
The Bags of Gold

Matthew 25:14-30

The three slaves stood to attention as their Master began to speak. They knew this was not an ordinary briefing of daily responsibilities for he had bought with him eight heavy bags of gold.

The Master was about to leave on a journey and was entrusting the three men standing there with running his business investments and resources. He'd been very successful, and by its wise use, his resources had kept increasing. It was no exaggeration to call the man fabulously wealthy ... and he was as generous as he was rich.

To one slave he gave five bags of gold - by some accounts the equivalent of 100 years income for an ordinary labourer! To another, two bags of gold and the remaining bag was handed to the third slave - in itself worth 20 years of wages for a common worker.

Insane!
Unbelievable!
No way!

These were the reactions of those listening to the Storyteller that day. The man in the story was over-the-top ridiculously generous, good and kind. But that was the reaction the Storyteller wanted; he wanted them to remember that they'd gasped incredulously. He continued his tale …

After a long time the Master returned, eager to learn how the three slaves had fared and decide what share of the profits should be credited to their accounts.

"Master," said the first slave, "you entrusted me with five bags of gold. See, I have gained five more."
"And you entrusted me with two," the second slave said, "and, I have gained two more."
"Well done!" the Master said, "you have been faithful with a few things; now I will put you in charge of many things. Come and share your master's happiness!"

There were more gasps of disbelief … the man in this story just called all that gold "a few things!" They could only imagine what sharing the Master's happiness might mean. They were awestruck at the magnitude of the man's wealth and generosity; they figured these slaves would now be set up with enough to run their own investment portfolios. However, their enjoyment of the story was about to take an unexpected turn.

"Master, I knew you were a harsh man, harvesting crops you didn't plant and gathering crops you didn't cultivate." The third slave was speaking. "I was afraid I would lose your gold, so I hid it in the earth. Look, here is your bag of gold back."

The Master was mortified ... "That's how you thought of me? That's who you perceived me to be? After working for me and being entrusted with so much, you were unable to see the heart of kindness that forgave debtors and only wanted good for all? You thought I was no better than the businessmen who stitched people up with contracts so they could take them to the cleaners over the slightest slip up?"

The first two slaves had an opposite perception of their Master. They knew him to be a kind and generous master ... and in the telling of this story there is nothing that suggests anything other than that. Because of their eagerness to participate in the Master's plan to create even more riches, and to share it even wider, he happily asked them to add this bag of gold to their own portfolios.

As for the slave who would not participate in his Master's joyful scheme, he went from bad to worse: unable to see good in anyone around him, suspicious of those over him and harsh toward his peers. His heart became ever darker, his life ever sadder, narrower. Whenever he saw the joy in his friends, his anger and frustration only increased. They lived in joy-giving light, and he, * the pain of a life collapsing from the inside.

* In most scripture translations: "outer darkness, where there will be weeping and gnashing of teeth."

"Grace is the celebration of life, relentlessly hounding all
the non-celebrants in the world. It is a floating, cosmic bash shouting its
way through the streets of the universe, flinging the sweetness of its
cassations to every window, pounding at every door in a hilarity beyond all
liking and happening, until the prodigals come out at last and dance, and
the elder brothers finally take their fingers out of their ears."

Robert Farrar Capon

The Storyteller's story of the Bags of Gold is more commonly known as the Parable of the Talents. It is the last section of the Olivet Discourse (Matthew 24 and 25), a sweeping response from Jesus to the question his disciples asked:

"Tell us, when will these things be (i.e. the collapse of every stone of the Temple), and what will be the sign of Your coming and of the end of the age (the final undoing of the Old Covenant age - the law age)?" (24:1-3)

Jesus had been clear - it would be that audience, that generation, who would see the fulfilment of this suite of warnings, prophecies and parables. (24:34)

For the next forty years believers (love slaves / servants of Jesus the Master) lived awestruck at the riches of the Master's grace, the endlessness of his loving kindness and the extravagance of his mercy. They shared it wherever they went and multitudes came to enjoy the freedom of living as the new creation they had become.

However, they were under severe duress to add Jewish law to their grace relationship with God and to return to the Temple, or at least to Temple observances. It was a seduction to believe the Master wasn't as generous or as trustworthy as they had first thought, that in fact he had a darker unpredictable cruel side. They should hedge their bets and incorporate the old with the new and live as they did before they had even heard of Christ.

This last story of the Olivet Discourse was Jesus' reiteration of the freedom and joy of living and participating in his full and overflowing grace. To know how spectacularly merciful and kind he would always be to them. It was a warning that the Temple Jews would try to seduce them back with an alternative narrative about him: of God with a merciless retributive side, who was hard and demanding.

The "outer darkness with weeping and anguish" was the destruction of Jerusalem and the Temple with massive loss of life that the Romans would bring upon the Jews. It would be the fate of all who lived there unless they managed a miraculous escape. The only people known to escape were those who believed and heeded the words of Jesus to be ready for his coming rescue.

I've come late to this scandalous grace party but I see it now: that my Master, the Lord of the whole earth, the Creator and Saviour of the human race is good, kind, trusting, happy and compassionate beyond any definition I could dare imagine - that he has no dark side. He is so to the whole world, whether rich or poor, frail or strong.

How was I able to live ... as a Christian ... without that incredulous gasp for so long!

During those days of visitation I came to know that our Master, Jesus Christ, is exactly what the Father, what the whole Trinity is like. The self-sacrificing love, the immeasurable mercy, his tenderness and rich graciousness is the essence of God in three persons. There is no angry God hiding behind the loving Jesus.

Barth and Billy

The great theologian of the twentieth century met the great evangelist of the twentieth century. When Billy Graham had visited Switzerland in 1960, he and Karl Barth got along very well. They met up twice, the second time in Barth's home in Basle.

But, "it was very different when we went to hear him let loose in the St Jacob stadium that same evening and witnessed his influence on the masses," Barth was to say, "I was quite horrified. What he presented was certainly not the gospel. It was the gospel at gun-point ... he preached the law ... he wanted to terrify people. Threats, they always make an impression ... The more one heats up hell ... the more they come running."

Barth was convinced that success did not justify such preaching. He considered it illegitimate to make the gospel law or, as he was to further say, "to push it like an article for sale ... We must leave the good God freedom to do his own work."

Soon after the days of my own encounter with the good and generous Master, I accepted his commission to spread his good news everywhere. I have decided to forsake a mixed gospel of grace and requirements, mercy and works, of forgiveness if I just meet the conditions.

I have chosen to participate in this new creation with total confidence in Jesus Christ, the Saviour of the world.

Mine is not the task of reconciling a fallen race to a loving God, that work has already been finished, there is no separation. My task is to tell people everywhere, to urge them to see and believe this stunning good news … to enable the blind to see what has been done by the kind and generous Master.

Brennan

Brennan Manning was a man who accepted "five bags of gold" from Jesus and invested the message of unconditional grace wherever he went. Brennan, a Catholic priest who became derelict through alcohol abuse, collided with the utter kindness of God and the riches of his grace and was transformed by it. Early in my journey in this more generous grace I memorized a beautiful set of questions from a sermon preached by Brennan:

> "Do you believe that the God of Jesus loves you beyond worthiness and unworthiness; beyond fidelity and infidelity; that he loves you in the morning sun and in the evening rain; that he loves you when your intellect denies it, your emotions refuse it, your whole being rejects it; do

you believe that God loves without condition or reservation, and loves you this moment as you are and not as you should be?"

I say 'yes' to these questions every day. They are my 'yes' to the invitation to imitate the Storyteller, to be a generous lover of all mankind.

Beloved St Paul from Tarsus
Mackenzie Phillips from The Shack
Father Robert Farrar Capon
The dead to whom Jesus descended on Holy Saturday
Mary Magdalene - the first Apostle (sent from the empty tomb)
Men and women from the last two thousand years - too many to count
Brennan Manning.

Suzanne and I joined the multitudes who had gasped incredulously ... living awestruck!

Selah
Pause | Consider | Apply

During a reading of Psalms (songs) the word Selah is included in the text to ask the singer to pause - a brief interlude to ponder the composition is being called for. Following each chapter of The Storyteller, you will find an invitation to "pause, consider and apply" - to personalise what you have just read by completing three intentionally open sentences. Alternatively, the Selah interlude can be used to trigger discussion and testimony in a group.

The Bags of Gold

Realising the extreme generosity of God has been …

How I perceive God to be has changed …

Living awestruck affects others around me …

Chapter Eight
Lazarus and the Rich Man

Luke 16:10-31

Poor Lazarus ate his last meal - scraps from the trash bag left outside a rich man's house. His only companions were the street dogs and whenever the rich man took out the trash, the dogs would scatter leaving Lazarus hoping he'd find a morsel to keep him alive another day.

The rich man loved money and he moved among friends with the same greed, including some of the religious big-wigs - they were exactly the same: lovers of money with no thought for the poor of their city.

The religious big-wigs would teach others about the after-life, that if they kept the required rituals and if they gave offerings of money for their house of worship, as well as offerings for the poor, they would go to a good and happy place when they died.

But they were dishonest hypocrites growing rich on the money in the offering boxes and passing none of it on to the poor.

One day a king from a far away place passed through their city. Some people were calling him the King of love because he was saying they must love their neighbours as themselves and be honest and kind with money. This king cared for the poor and those despised by others but he got nothing but ridicule from the religious big-wigs because they were greedy and heartless; nothing like this king.

These hypocrites had pushed from their own conscience what they taught others - that the greedy, the dishonest, those who despised the poor would be tormented in the grave, burning up in the agony of regret for the lives they'd lived. It was a handy teaching for prising cash from the wallets of their hearers, as they just continued to build their personal wealth.

One day the good king turned to the religious big-wigs and told them that poor Lazarus had died and had been carried by angels to that good and happy place. The hypocrites were puzzled by this because they hadn't seen Lazarus making offerings for a very long time.

Then the king told them that their rich friend had also died and was now suffering the fate they had once told would be the lot of those who despised the poor. The good king was taking their very teaching about the afterlife and throwing it back at them, exposing their hypocrisy in front of all the ordinary people whom they had conned.

He told his stunned hearers that nothing could be done to relieve the greedy man's pain and that Abraham - the keeper of the good and happy place - told him that a great chasm separated them in the grave, just like the chasm between the greedy and the poor whilst living. The king wanted them to know the virtue of crossing the divide between rich and poor, now in this life, of choosing love - but that to refuse compassion, to become so familiar with lovelessness would become a torment from which only love could save.

"I ask myself: What is hell?"
And I answer thus: "The suffering of being
no longer able to love."

Fyodor Dostoevsky (The Brothers Karamazov)

I made a big mistake with this story from the great Storyteller. I thought it was a story from which to teach about the afterlife. It just didn't occur to me that it was a story about greed and kindness, religious hypocrisy and sincere compassion.

I was much later to learn that the concept of the afterlife in this story was developed well after the Jewish Torah, the Psalms and Prophets of the Bible. It was an idea taken from the Greeks and Egyptians and developed in Israel during the four centuries between the Testaments (the period in which the cult of the Pharisees came into prominence).

By the time Jesus comes on the scene, Temple ministry was a farce of hypocrisy denounced as a "den of thieves" as he drove out the money men from its sacred courts. Their rendition of what lay beyond the grave was nothing but a manipulative tool by which they enriched themselves. A technique emulated by the Popes of the sixteenth century who sold indulgences - credits that could be used to reduce one's time in purgatory. It had outraged Martin Luther but in this story, it was Jesus who was confronting greed and lovelessness.

Try as I may, I could no longer regard the Storyteller's telling of Lazarus and the rich man as his endorsement of a version of hell known as eternal conscious torment. The context didn't allow it to be interpreted that way nor did the weight of Biblical revelation.

If I took the beautiful child from Papamoa Beach (chapter 3) and placed her where the rich man was in this story - took out an eternal conscious torment lens of interpretation through which to view it - what I'd see would be an utter travesty.

If I placed a dear, close member of my family there - someone who had shown kindness to others all her life, yet had never raised her hand at the appeal of an evangelist, nor prayed his prayer - it was a hideous repudiation of all I had come to know of the loving Trinity both by study and experience.

There's another occasion when the great Storyteller pictured religious big-wigs in fiery judgment - he called them goats. Why did they end up in such trouble? Was it because they had failed to receive Jesus as their personal Saviour? No! It was because when they saw the hungry they didn't feed them. When they saw the refugee they refused to welcome them. They would not clothe the naked, take care of the sick, nor would they visit those in prison. They wouldn't cross chasms.

Theirs was "the suffering of being no longer able to love."

Crossing Chasms

Chasms are unknown in the Trinity. It's why we say they are Three and they are One. We also say They are love - St John said that and we do well to repeat it every day.

God is a relationship of other-centred love.

All of us have been created for love and relationship; by Love and Relationship Himself! Everything comes from God, so love and relationship are what gives meaning to the Universe and meaning to our lives. It's the supreme point of life and living.

Interesting isn't it that from the smallest atom with particles circling and spinning, to distant Galaxies where stars and planets and moons circle and spin on a vast scale … it's a relational Universe; we have a world where everything works beautifully when in right relationship.

This, of course, is true not just in the material world and world of nature, it is true for human life as well.

If near their death, a person is asked concerning any regrets they have, seldom will they speak of achievement, acquisition or accomplishment - but frequently they will say how they wish they had given more priority and time to their relationships with family and others; and to have lived at a less hurried pace in order to do so.

St Paul magnifies love as much as Jesus; he places it above the extraordinary realm of prophetic seeing and mountain moving faith … "Love is the greatest: and it will never fail" Paul enthuses.

As I have had a growing understanding and experience of the essence of God, I've wanted to be like God - full of loving kindness. Maybe I'm getting there. At least I know that a lot of things that were once important to me, things from which I, perhaps, had derived meaning and value are far less important to me now.

I know what it is to have others love me. I know how uplifting, how healing and assuring it feels. What a gift to let overflow to others. To put our relationships before all else. To close a chasm.

All the broken and dislocated pieces of the universe.

There's a stunning rendition in the Message Bible of Paul's vision of God's plan to redeem and restore, through Jesus Christ, every relationship that's been broken, that's fallen from the unity and harmony they had in the creation of all things. Two verses from Colossians chapter one that powerfully confirm that this is a relational universe. Paul writes concerning Jesus:

"So spacious is he, so roomy, that everything of God finds its proper place in him without crowding. Not only that, but all the broken and dislocated pieces of the universe - people and things, animals and atoms - get properly fixed and fit together in vibrant harmonies, all because of his death, his blood that poured down from the cross." (Colossians 1:18-20 MSG)

We come from perfect connection, perfect union and shared joy ... deepest in us is the memory and yearning for this highest of all experiences. We're wired for caring affection, not for chasms - break a circuit, pull adrift a connection and life doesn't work. Nothing works, nothing starts, nothing runs smoothly - it's hell.

Our friends, Stuart and Jenny, visited Barcelona in 2018 and were awestruck by the magnificent La Sagrada Familia cathedral that's been under construction for the past 136 years. I was taken by this quote from the brilliant and devout architect, Antoni Gaudi, that they shared with me - he said, "To do things right, first you need love, then technique."

Life has no meaning outside of our pursuit of love, harmony, unity and relationship with the whole created world of people, of nature - of all things. If you don't mind me saying so, the point of life is not to get to heaven and to ensure as many people as you can persuade get there too, no! The point of life is to experience heaven here and now: that the beautiful and harmonious affection that flows between the Father, Son and Spirit, is flowing into our world from our lives every day!

Yes, everything and everyone around us is wired for love and relationship. O what love has exploded out from God - the One they called the King of love - the One who crossed every chasm to find us, include us, dwell in us and cause us to sit together with him, holy and blameless, inside the circle of Divine affection.

The Pharisees, the religious big-wigs, had altogether failed to comprehend the meaning of life. That the universe works by relationship, by crossing chasms, by loving kindness.

"What is hell?" Elder Zosima asks himself in Dostoevsky's classic book: "The suffering of being no longer able to love" he replies.

Selah
Pause | Consider | Apply

During a reading of Psalms (songs) the word Selah is included in the text to ask the singer to pause - a brief interlude to ponder the composition is being called for. Following each chapter of The Storyteller, you will find an invitation to "pause, consider and apply" - to personalise what you have just read by completing three intentionally open sentences. Alternatively, the Selah interlude can be used to trigger discussion and testimony in a group.

Lazarus and the Rich Man

The parable of Lazarus and the rich man challenges me to ...

If the rich man represents the world I live in, the attitudes Jesus would confront are ...

My hope is that the love that flows out from the Trinity, flows through me to ...

Chapter Nine
The Good Samaritan

Luke 10:25-37

Thud! One last blow landed on the man's head. The thieves had taken everything, even his clothing, then fled, leaving him for dead in the middle of nowhere.

In those days, most people walked from town to town, sometimes they would ride a donkey or a camel. First on the scene came a priest on foot but he gave the man a wide berth. Coincidentally, the next traveller to pass by was another priest - from a different order - and although the beaten man lifted his hand to beckon for help, this priest too, rushed by.

Later that day a traveller from the north ... (the Storyteller's audience of one, a lawyer, visibly squirmed. The northerners were dangerous fanatics, their religion abhorrent and their history that of scumbags ... or so the story had been told ... northerners and southerners simply didn't talk or deal with each other).

The northerner was moved with pity and went to the beaten man's aid. He applied healing lotions as he bandaged the stranger's wounds. Carefully he lifted him onto his donkey which he led to the next tavern, hired a room and took care of him overnight. The following day he paid the tavern owner in advance for the lodgings as well as to care for the man until he returned from his trip.

The Storyteller stopped and asked the Lawyer, "Which of these three was a good neighbour to the man who had been left for dead on the road?" The answer should have been easy but the answer came only after an awkward pause ... "The one who showed him mercy," came the difficult reply.

"'Does that mean,' said Mack, 'that all roads lead to you?'
'Not at all.' Jesus smiled as he reached for the door handle to the shop.
'Most roads don't lead anywhere. What it does mean is that I will travel
any road to find you.'"

Wm. Paul Young (The Shack)

The Samaritans occupied territory once part of Israel. When the ten tribes of Israel were carried into captivity, the king of Assyria sent people from other nations to inhabit Samaria and these foreigners intermarried with the Israelite population.

The Samaritans, therefore, embraced a culture that was a mixture of Judaism and the worship of idols. Furthermore, the Samaritans built their own temple, insisting it was designated by Moses as the place where the nation should worship.

So the Jews regarded the Samaritans as the worst of the human race and had no dealings with them.

The Samaritans were racially different from the Jews.
They were religiously abhorrent to the Jews.
They did not have the same moral/sexual boundaries as the Jews.
The Samaritans had displaced two of Israel's tribes from their inheritance.

And then three Samaritan stories weave themselves into the story of Jesus. The great Storyteller was confronting Samariaphobia.

15 March 2019

On Friday the 15th March 2019 I was sitting in the airport terminal awaiting my flight to Palmerston North. I had been invited to speak at the Sunday services of a church in the region. Soon after 2.00pm small crowds started to gather around the television monitors in the terminal departure lounge.

News was breaking of a tragedy unfolding in Christchurch in New Zealand's south. A gunman had entered two Mosques brandishing a semi-automatic weapon and gunned down men, women and children during Friday prayers. By the time the scenes had been secured and the gunman captured, fifty one people lay dead, either on the floor where they had prayed or in the hospital to which they had been rushed.

During my short flight and through the next day, my mind was on one thing ... the collective mind of five million Kiwis was on one thing and we tuned into every news bulletin for more information. This was New Zealand's 9/11 except this had been a hate crime perpetrated upon Muslims, not by them.

It seemed life had changed for all of us, and most certainly my ministry plans for Sunday had to change.

A voice I had come to know well - the voice from the Heavenly Three - "They are your Samaritans."

During our years in Fiji, Suzanne and I had developed a sincere affection for the many Muslim friends we made. They were peace loving, family oriented, hard working people devoted to their faith. They showed us hospitality and care that kept us immune from the Islamophobia that we'd seen rising in many parts of the Church as well as in Western society in general.

When I heard "They are your Samaritans", I believed I was being asked to give voice to the story of the Samaritans and the graciously accepting Son, and relate it to our divisions and phobias towards different others. To face up to the "othering".

The Voice was right. On the whole, our society and the Christian believers in it had no dealings with this community of immigrant refugees: we didn't care for their religion, their cultural differences and the violence others who prayed to this Allah had perpetrated in some parts of the world … "They are your Samaritans."

The lawyer's dis-ease in the Storyteller's story was not difficult to relate to. Casting a Samaritan as the good guy, the hero in this story was an audacious move. Moments earlier the conversation had flowed like this …

Lawyer: "Teacher, what must I do to inherit eternal life?"

Jesus: "What is written in the law? What do you read there?"

Lawyer: "You shall love the Lord your God with all your heart, and with all your soul, and with all your strength, and with all your mind; and your neighbour as yourself."

Jesus: "You have given the right answer; do this, and you will live."

Lawyer: "And who is my neighbour?"

Jesus: "A man was going down from Jerusalem to Jericho, and fell into the hands of robbers …" (Luke 10:25-30)

Awkward.

The Samaritans were the Jew's northern neighbours. Jesus is saying "Love the one you hate the most."

Soon after this, Jesus heals ten lepers but only one of them returns and thanks him. Luke records this story and he especially notes the thankful leper was a … Samaritan! However, we're not told the nationalities of the other lepers, just this one … who the Jews despised.

Why tell us he's a Samaritan? To tell us that the people we despise the most have hearts that beat just like ours. To move us toward a more generous inclusion. To dismantle our Samariaphobias.

The third story is the one we know about the woman at the well. Jesus does something the Jews wouldn't do - travel through Samaria. His conversation with the woman was neither harsh nor alienating, instead it was including and without condemnation. This woman was to become one of great influence, through whom many came to experience the living water of love and grace from its very source.

"I will travel any road to find you."

Lost & Found

Lost & Found is a television series in which families are reunited after fascinating detective work by the host of the show. Whilst watching an episode I realised - this is God! - this is the story of all stories being played out one family at a time. The God story of reconciliation.

I realised there could be an episode of Lost & Found of a family that got split up when half of them were dragged off as slaves by a foreign army. Then those who remained, intermarried with people of foreign cultures and eventually became a different people of mixed-blood, a new religion - and a new ID - Samaritans.

Then when the members of that family finally returned from their captivity instead of seeking to find and embrace the relatives they had been separated from, they saw their difference and despised them.

This went on for generations, until ... just one member of that divided family was able to think differently because he knew the Heavenly Father was not a bit like the sin-conscious, judgement threatening God the rest of his family believed.

Just one member of the family crossed the gaping prejudice of 1000 years. Jesus sat down at a well and told a broken lady about the generosity of God.

"I will travel any road to find you."

They are us

The victims of the massacre on 15th March were mostly from families who had come to New Zealand seeking a peaceful life, many had come from strife-torn parts of the world as refugees. It seemed to make our sense of national angst all the more poignant.

On this dark day, our Prime Minister, in the course of addressing the nation, inserted three words into a communication that had been prepared by her staff for a press conference. Of the dead, injured, bereaved family and close knit immigrant community she said to all New Zealanders - "They are us."

It was a simple and defining statement of manaakitanga (in the Māori language: hospitality, kindness, generosity, acceptance and adoption) toward those who at one time lived their lives in another part of the world ... but now ... "They are us."

The ability to rid myself of fearful and exclusive thinking concerning different others, whether that difference was cultural, religious, colour or gender-related, had been challenging for me prior to my Fiji experience and subsequent encounter with God. I understood how many in the Church readily rejected the idea that "They are us."

Before calling upon the Athenians to turn their thinking around (Athens was a city full of diverse religious shrines and practices) St Paul affirmed that they were the very offspring of God. That, just as with himself, they lived in Christ, moved and had their being in him; the loving Trinity was not far from any of them. (Acts 17).

It's universal! Nothing and no one escapes the embrace, the reconciling love of God.

The day after Friday the 15th of March 2019, the God and Father of all said, "They are your Samaritans." It was an invitation from above to participate in the radical acceptance that flows inside the Trinity and out into the universe of their creation An invitation to be a generous lover of all mankind.

In his book, 'Conjectures of a Guilty Bystander', Thomas Merton writes of the moment he saw humanity through the eyes of God.

"In Louisville, at the corner of Fourth and Walnut, in the center of the shopping district, I was suddenly overwhelmed with the realisation that I loved all these people, that they were mine and I theirs, that we could not be alien to one another even though we were total strangers. It was like waking from a dream of separateness, of spurious self-isolation, in a special world.

"This sense of liberation from an illusory difference was such a relief and such a joy to me that I almost laughed out loud ... I have the immense joy of being man, a member of a race in which God Himself became incarnate. As if the sorrows and stupidities of the human condition could overwhelm me, now that I realise what we all are. And if only everybody could realise this! But it cannot be explained. There is no way of telling people that they are all walking around shining like the sun.

"Then it was as if I suddenly saw the secret beauty of their hearts, the depths of their hearts where neither sin nor desire nor self-knowledge can reach, the core of their reality, the person that each one is in God's eyes. If only they could all see themselves as they really are. If only we could see each other that way all the time."

(Thomas Merton - Conjectures of a Guilty Bystander
Bantam Doubleday Bell Publishing Group Inc.
1 April 1994)

Selah
Pause | Consider | Apply

During a reading of Psalms (songs) the word Selah is included in the text to ask the singer to pause - a brief interlude to ponder the composition is being called for. Following each chapter of The Storyteller, you will find an invitation to "pause, consider and apply" - to personalise what you have just read by completing three intentionally open sentences. Alternatively, the Selah interlude can be used to trigger discussion and testimony in a group.

The Good Samaritan

The people group phobia that's challenged me the most is ...

What has helped me unconditionally embrace the different other is ...

I stand in awe of God who ...

Chapter Ten
The Unforgiving Servant

Matthew 18:23-35

"Pay me ... now!" the servant demanded with threats of violence. He was owed ten dollars.

His debtor's reaction was the same as had just been played out before the king, the servant pleading for a chance to pay back what he owed - one hundred thousand dollars! The king had mercy and forgave his servant the gigantic debt, but no such forgiveness was coming for the one who owed the forgiven servant just ten. "Throw him in jail until the money is paid!"

The king was abhorred when he heard that the servant, who he had just forgiven a colossal debt, had shown no mercy to one whose debt was so tiny by comparison. He ordered that the unforgiving servant be tormented until he paid back his entire debt.

The Storyteller turned to his small audience; they were hanging on his every word. "Unforgiveness will torment anyone who holds it in their heart, you must forgive everyone, unconditionally, to be truly free."

"To forgive is to set someone free,
and then find out that it's you."

Rob Bell (The Robcast Episode 38)

The Storyteller had two vital truths he wanted his followers to hear. The first concerned the unparalleled generosity of the King's mercy revealed by the unconditional forgiveness he extends to even the most serious offender.

The second concerned the prison of torment an unforgiving person locks themselves into when they harbour resentments and judgements against others.

Quite early in the days of the experience that so radically changed my life, I became troubled by the picture of an angry God of punishment, mercilessly subjecting his only son to pay, through excruciating torture and death, the debt for the sins and offenses committed by you and me. In theology this is called 'penal substitutionary atonement' (atonement meaning 'to make at one' - practically the same as 'reconciliation').

This picture was an out of character distortion of the heavenly Father I had come to know; and of the relationship within the Trinity from which all goodness flowed. It also clashed with St Paul's assertion that God was in Christ reconciling the world to himself - not detached from Jesus, but meeting the world "in" him. Paul's next statement reveals the means by which reconciliation took place … "not counting people's sins against them" (2 Corinthians 5:19 NIV).

There's a single word for that ... forgiveness.

[In chapters 5 and 6, I discussed the question "Why did Jesus have to die?" Taking the death penalty, meted out by an angry God, as a substitute for you and me is not one of them].

I once was taught that someone has to be punished for there to be reconciliation, or at-one-ment. Yet those who taught me that, would never say that to a couple with a broken relationship (at least I hope not). No, they would say, that deep, self-less and unconditional forgiveness will heal this marriage and restore the relationship. When that's between God and the human race, it's news that is unimaginably good!

You cannot have unconditional forgiveness, then add a condition for justice to be served. There's nothing just about indiscriminate forgiveness ... it's simply love like we've never seen before, on a scale we can't comprehend.

God's radical, free and unconditional forgiveness has reconciled the world to himself. We are in union with Trinity, adopted into the heavenly places of Father, Son and Spirit, holy and blameless before him. As soon as we see that, all striving ceases, God appeasement is no more. Love, peace and joy start rising within us and we find the invitation to participate in the forgiving flow irresistible.

An Apology

I put down the phone and said to Suzanne, "Guess who just invited us to lunch?" She made a few attempts before I told her. I told her carefully because she had been deeply hurt by this man. We'd both been through a painful experience with him but it was Suzanne who wept everyday for months as all the pain and anxiety of the experience made its way out of her.

The table was nicely set and we sat around it with the man and his wife. He asked for blessing upon the food and as soon as the Amen's had been said he placed his hands on the table, looked us in the eye and said, "David and Sue, I want to ask your forgiveness, I want to apologise for ..." and he reiterated the offence that had alienated us for many years.

Because years had passed, the impact of the offence had lessened and we seldom thought of it. We had forgiven him in the way that one does without having to confront him. However, it was only following our act of forgiveness around the lunch table that the separation came to an end, the relationship was healed and reconciliation became a reality.

As we drove home I commented to Sue how much respect for him I was starting to feel once again. I knew that by stepping into that flow of forgiveness I was now free to speak well of him to others and to fellowship with him free from intimidation.

To forgive is to set someone free, and then find out that it's you.

The Thief on the Cross

"But what about the thieves being crucified on either side of Jesus? He forgave one but he didn't forgive the other."

I quietly sighed ... why do people want a Jesus who is less generous, one who is a stickler for protocol, needing us to tick a few pre-conditional boxes before he forgives? Why can't we just have love without limits, grace without measure and mercy that triumphs over judgment?

"Let's think about this," I slowly replied to buy a bit of time before attempting a response that would calm my challenger down (how dare I suggest a God, a love, that keeps no record of wrongs, who doesn't forgive because we prayed the right prayer but because he is perfect mercy).

"The Bible's account of the exchange doesn't tell us that Jesus refused to forgive the cranky thief," I offered. "Do you remember how that soon after his conversation with the two thieves, Jesus is asking his Father to forgive his torturers, his murderers and the religious plotters who handed him over to the Romans for execution?" (Luke 23:39-43) "Do you think if Jesus forgave them - none of whom sought his forgiveness or prayed any kind of prayer - do you think the thief's crimes were harder for God to pardon, that he wouldn't extend mercy to this man too?"

"But ..."

I continued, "If Paul is to be believed, both thieves and all the evil men from that day and place were joined to Christ in his dying; they were part of the 'world' that was being forgiven and reconciled to God on that day of all days."

I took a quick breath, "If the cranky thief wasn't included there, then we're agreeing that God has chosen some for salvation and he's chosen others for damnation. That's called Hyper-Calvinism, and I'm sorry, but I reject all loveless theology."

My blood of the covenant

Every Sunday at Commoners Church we celebrate and remember something staggering! A covenant relationship made real through a broken body and by shed blood.

During the Eucharist each person is given a piece of bread broken from a common loaf which we dip in a common cup of wine. We eat and we drink, we experience Presence and we affirm our eternal gratitude.

When this simple meal was first instituted, Jesus Christ said "this is my blood of the covenant, which is poured out for many for the forgiveness of sins." (Matthew 26:27-28 NIV).

I often buy books online - sometimes to be delivered to friends. As the purchase is being completed, I am required to do two important things: choose the delivery address and pay the required sum. This completes the purchase.

On the cross, a new covenant was being inaugurated. It was making obsolete an old covenant through which the nation of Israel related to God by the keeping of laws and ritual sacrifices. The new covenant is for the whole world; through the broken body and shed blood, and then resurrection, of Christ, we are ushered into his relationship with his Father - a new creation, marked by forgiveness.

Jesus Christ, the Saviour of the world, first chose the delivery address to whom the unconditional forgiveness, the new creation and the covenant relationship with his Father would be delivered. He co-joined himself with you and me and the whole human family through the incarnation. It would cost him his life, his blood would be spilt ... but "for the joy that was set before him endured the cross, disregarding its shame, and has taken his seat at the right hand of the throne of God" (Hebrews 12:2).

He didn't let us go for a moment, but seated us together with him in the heavenly places. Payment made. Delivery completed. Finished!

Baxter's Boys

For one day in 2014, Suzanne and I were privileged to host Paul Young and Baxter Kruger - two wonderful storytellers. We hired a large country lodge, invited thirty fellow pilgrims and soaked in the Trinitarian love and grace that flowed from these men.

It was there that Baxter told of the time he was working at his desk when two shadowy figures in battle dress appeared at his office door. He knew what was coming. Suddenly his young son rushed across the room and leapt on his father. Both Baxter and his son wrestled to the floor in mock battle. Moments later his son's friend, a boy quite unknown to Baxter, joined the play flight.

Before long, both boys retreated and Baxter was left thinking, "Now there's a boy with real boldness, play fighting with his friend's Dad; someone he'd not met before." At that moment, Baxter said, the Lord spoke to him, "Baxter, pay attention to what just happened." Then it was obvious, the boy would never have done that had he been alone; but here he was entering the relationship the father's son had with his Dad.

Jesus is the new covenant, a relationship for the whole world secured by blood and remembered by bread and wine. I don't have a personal relationship with God to secure and maintain. Jesus is my relationship with God - and it's perfect!

> I have given you as a covenant to the people,
> a light to the nations,
> To open the eyes that are blind,
> to bring out the prisoners from the dungeon,
> from the prison those who sit in darkness.
> I am the LORD, that is my name;
> my glory I give to no other, nor my praise to idols.
> See, the former things have come to pass,
> and new things I now declare;
> before they spring forth,
> I tell you of them.
> Sing to the LORD a new song,
> his praise from the end of the earth!
> (Isaiah 42:6-10)

We've been called to participate in the radical forgiveness that flowed to us from the Saviour of the world. To forgive as we have been forgiven. An invitation to be a generous lover of all mankind. Imagine the transformation that would take place if this forgiving flow became the norm in the smallest families, all the way through to the political world of international relationships!

G.K. Chesterton wisely prods us ... "The Christian ideal has not been tried and found wanting. It has been found difficult; and left untried."

Selah
Pause | Consider | Apply

During a reading of Psalms (songs) the word Selah is included in the text to ask the singer to pause - a brief interlude to ponder the composition is being called for. Following each chapter of The Storyteller, you will find an invitation to "pause, consider and apply" - to personalise what you have just read by completing three intentionally open sentences. Alternatively, the Selah interlude can be used to trigger discussion and testimony in a group.

The Unforgiving Servant

I knew that I had been unconditionally forgiven when ...

For me, the invitation to participate in the forgiving flow is ...

Words I would use to describe the truth that Jesus is my relationship with God ...

Chapter Eleven
The Ten Bridesmaids

Matthew 25:1-13

With invitations in one hand and lamps in the other, the ten young women made their way to the evening celebrations of their friend's wedding. The husband-to-be was coming in a colourful and noisy procession; the banquet room was being readied for the happy occasion.

However, the bridegroom's procession was delayed so the young women extinguished their lamps and settled down to rest. Soon they were all fast asleep.

With a cacophony of drums, musical instruments, lights and colourful banners, the bridegroom's procession coming from a distance woke the young women. They hurriedly reached for their lamps.

Five of the ten realised they would not have enough oil to fuel the lamps for the duration of the night. Quickly they went to find oil and buy what they needed.

However, before they returned, the bridegroom's party arrived at the banquet. Five young women whose lamps were in no danger of going out went into the feast.

The five who had the dimming lamps eventually returned but found the doors to the banquet firmly closed and they were shut out from the celebration they had so looked forward to enjoying with their friends.

The Storyteller's story of the Ten Bridesmaids is from a suite of warnings, prophecies and parables known as the Olivet Discourse (Matthew 24 and 25), a sweeping response from Jesus to the question his disciples asked:

"Tell us, when will these things be (i.e. the collapse of every stone of the Temple) and what will be the sign of Your coming and of the end of the age (the final undoing of the Old Covenant age - the law age)?" (24:1-3)

Jesus had been clear: it would be that audience, that generation, who would see the fulfilment of these narratives that concerned this critical time in the nation's history. (24:34)

They had encountered Jesus, the light of the world, and forsook the dim religion of laws and sacrifices that had dominated their lives. They were free, their eyes had been opened and, despite the daily hardships of life in their occupied land, they were happy that it no longer included strict adherence to the myriad of requirements they had once believed were necessary to be pleasing to God.

However some, for different reasons, were vulnerable to opposition and persecution. It was as if the illuminating wonder of encountering the Saviour and experiencing his grace and truth was not the only reason they joined the ranks of believers. They started with 'less in the tank' than most of their friends.

As the years rolled on, the duress from the old religion to return to the Temple increased. For those who had been filled with the light of the gospel and lived awestruck at the riches of God's grace, to resist the pressure was easy, their 'tank was full.' But for those with 'less awe in the tank', they hadn't completely changed their minds about their Jewish religion and thought they could save themselves a lot of pain by just returning and mixing Temple law in with the grace of God.

This story in the Olivet Discourse was a warning of the pressuring persecution to come; and it was encouragement for the believers to gaze in the metaphorical mirror and see the radiant new creation they had become.

In its setting, the story made it clear that time was running out, that if they clung to the Temple their lives were in danger; they risked missing the One speeding to their rescue.

Bull-Riding Bill

It was Bill's first time in our Sunday church service; in fact I learned that Bill only ever darkened the door of a church for weddings and funerals. He'd been befriended by a member of our congregation and sat close to the front taking in all that was happening during the service.

Folk had greeted Bill warmly, I guess most had never met someone who had made a living from riding bulls. Retired now, after a career with hard-living men and never in one place for too long when on the rodeo circuit, he was not short of an interesting yarn. Bill was obviously feeling quite at home because as I was closing the service he raised his hand, "Excuse me, excuse me, may I say something?" he asked.

I was not practiced at handling unexpected requests from strangers to say something that the whole church would likely hear. It was risky was it not? But I replied, "Certainly Bill, please go ahead."

Bill stood up and looked around, looked back at me and said, "I've never felt love like this before," with a quaver in his voice, "I've never been here before, but I can feel love here." With that he sat back down, if I remember correctly to some applause and affirmations from the rest of the congregation.

Bill had met love in the person of Jesus Christ, invisibly present in the lives of the people he'd interacted with that morning. It instantly changed his thinking about God and himself. That was in 2013 and Bill has gone from faith to faith ever since. That morning, Bill started to see what had been true about him all along.

Through this journey on these high seas, Suzanne and I started to understand that the overriding narrative of the Apostles was not about personal sin and unrighteousness but about beholding light, about seeing, about believing and about thinking differently. We were recognising that the greatest force for personal transformation and healing is encountering the radiance of God and seeing the glorious newness that already defines our life in Christ.

We saw that our inclusion in Christ's reconciling work was one thing, but that seeing, believing and therefore participating in the wonder of it was something else again - it would be transformative. If we're alienated from the love-saturated Trinity, then it's in our minds - but not in truth (Colossians 1:19-22).

Perhaps that's what made the difference between the young women in the Storyteller's story. Five had encountered the luminous Christ and knew that he had taken away every shadow of sin (as the angel Gabriel and John the Baptist announced he would). The other five still had a 'recording' from the Temple playing in their heads: messages about sin and judgment, separation from God, about not doing enough.

We were grieved every time we heard "sin" sermons in churches we visited. The sin-consciousness among preachers seemed to be telling us how little they knew about the new covenant and the transforming power of believing. It was a narrative far more suited to the Temple, not the Church.

Quite simply, the Old Covenant reveals what's wrong, mis-formed and flawed; and it is preoccupied with behaviour modification.

The New Covenant reveals what's new, redeemed and glorious; it is preoccupied with believing the beauty of Christ's image within.

Narnia

C.S. Lewis places "a little band of scowling dwarfs" right in the middle of the glory that is Narnia. They're scowling and bad tempered because "there's something wrong with their eyes" and they can't see the splendid beauty about them, nor could they taste the deliciousness of either food or wine.

The problem is not that the Dwarfs have been excluded from the glory of Narnia but that their eyes are wrong. The absence of proper seeing leaves them incapable of experiencing Narnia as Narnia.

The Mirror

Biblical scholar François DuToit's Mirror Study Bible is a masterpiece of new creation awareness, look what I found in St Paul's second letter to the Corinthians:

> "Gazing with wonder at the loveliness of God displayed
> in human form, we suddenly realize that we are looking
> into a mirror, where every feature of his image articulated
> in Christ is reflected within us!" (3:18 Mirror)

The "loveliness of God" is the Greek word "doxa", elsewhere translated "the glory of God."

Earlier in the passage (Chapter 3), Paul has written about both the old and the new covenants. The first, he tells us, has a glory that's fading away. The second, has a lasting and surpassing glory. Having discussed the differences between the two, Paul invites us to a mirror.

It's not complicated ... When we look in a mirror we see ourselves. I see me! It's scandalous! We see ourselves and we see the glory of God! We see the loveliness of God displayed in the person reflected there. No, it's not talking about the Bible, neither is it any other kind of beholding, gazing or looking. When I see me, I see the glory of God! And here's what Paul goes on to say: we ...

> " ... are being changed into the same image from glory to glory, even as by the Spirit of the Lord."
> (2 Corinthians 3:18 KJV)

This is what gives us a continually full tank that will illuminate our lives; we can be the five wise young women in the Storyteller's parable.

Beautiful Holy Spirit is there
with you
at the mirror,
taking what's true about you in the new creation,
touching you so that your spiritual reality becomes your conscious reality in life.

That person of love and mercy you see in the mirror is the person people meet everyday!

I once taught that our transformation was from glory to glory to glory to glory, as if Paul is talking about some long progressive process, but there are only two "glories" in Paul's statement: the fading glory of the old covenant and the surpassing glory. That's it, just two, exactly as he told it.

What's powerful here is that Paul is saying God has already created you anew, he doesn't have you on a slow-drip of change. Here's the change: you died and you rose again!

What's gradual here, is getting over our reluctance to see what's really being reflected in that mirror and saying "I see me, I see the glory of God!" That's the truth that the five wise maidens knew ...

"A butterfly is treasured for its intricate, beautiful design and colour. Yet a butterfly cannot see the glory of its wings ... until it happens upon a mirror." (Anon)

... Like a butterfly they had landed on a mirror and had seen the glory with which they were truly involved.

The Storyteller is telling that generation of believers something crucial. And it's so very important for us as well. Keep going back to the mirror and take your friends there, take the broken there, take those who have never seen anything good about themselves. Take them to the mirror - Holy Spirit will be there - and start to tell them (tell yourself) the new creation, the glory, the loveliness you see.

As we sailed on in this journey of grace, we were not only encountering a new startling vision of God, but also of our own intrinsic value and loveliness. What a utter joy to participate in the kindness and transforming goodness that flows inside the Trinity and out to every man, woman, boy and girl ... to have a new story to tell, to be their light, the illuminator of what's amazing about who they became when God joined them to Jesus and adopted them as his own dear children.

Selah
Pause | Consider | Apply

During a reading of Psalms (songs) the word Selah is included in the text to ask the singer to pause - a brief interlude to ponder the composition is being called for. Following each chapter of The Storyteller, you will find an invitation to "pause, consider and apply" - to personalise what you have just read by completing three intentionally open sentences. Alternatively, the Selah interlude can be used to trigger discussion and testimony in a group.

The Ten Bridesmaids

For some, seeing themselves in the new covenant is a process, and for me ...

To be free from sin-consciousness and alive to my new self has meant ...

I love the idea of the mirror because ...

Chapter Twelve
The Great Commission

Matthew 28:16-20

Eleven disciples practically ran up the mountain above Lake Galilee - their Master, Jesus, had said he'd meet them there. The image of his body being laid in the Garden tomb was still playing in their minds, but not as brightly as the one the women had 'painted' of the tomb completely empty and the Master ... alive and talking with them there.

There were other scenes, too, where Jesus had shown up, the marks of his torturous execution visible on his body. Now this instruction: "Meet me on the mountain above the lake." Why wouldn't they be running?

These men, picked out from ordinary lives, had just enjoyed the three most incredible years with the Master: the love, the laughter, the camaraderie of this band of brothers. They were caught up in a whirlwind of miracles; of sheer wonder; of courage-demanding moments; of the most amazing fellowship with Jesus.

Jesus had been a calm, assuring and commanding presence during those heady days. The turmoil of nature, human tragedy and religious skulduggery meant there was never a dull moment. Sometimes they feared for their very lives but there was Jesus in the middle of it all, never fazed and equipped to handle any situation.

The eleven were still catching their breath as he went around hugging and slapping them lovingly. "I've not lost anything, in fact, I'm holding everything," Jesus began to say, "I have all the keys! Heaven and earth, the world and the underworld - all the keys!" He was excited and calm at the same time, if that's possible. The eleven knew he had a handle on everything, even if they didn't, and a powerful sense of authority, kingliness, could be felt even when he was clowning around with them on the mountain, above the lake.

Then Jesus says, "keep bringing people from all over the world into what we've had, what we've got." And adds, "and don't forget, I am with you to the very end, always! This happy life with me and one another doesn't get interrupted and it will never end, it's 24/7."

The eleven looked at one another and said, almost in unison … "Wow! this is a great commission!"

Jesus was saying, "keep bringing people from all over the world into what we've had and it'll be as presence-filled for them as it was around the shores of Galilee with me."

"That'll be easy, who wouldn't want a life of fellowship with the happy God … and with us!" (and they were right). Just like the eleven, everyone who joined them immersed themselves in this happy band and became God-learners (it's what 'disciple' means).

On the mountain above the lake Jesus had one more thing to add. He said it knowing that to the eleven it hardly needed saying but his words would still be talked about centuries later, so he said it hoping, longing, its power and utter simplicity would not be lost …

"All those you bring into this from all over the world; teach them … love." He took a breath, "teach them to love God, to love their fellow man, to love themselves and to love all the other God-learners."

The eleven looked at each other, then looked at Jesus. This time they did say it in unison: "Wow! this is a great commission!"

Then they all rolled on the ground laughing.

"In eternity past, the Godhead purposes to one day expand
its fellowship to a people not yet created ... to produce a community
on earth that will reflect the community that is found among the
Father, the Son, and the Spirit."

Frank Viola (The Untold Story of the New Testament Church)

As my pilgrimage in this more generous grace continued I became more convinced of how desperately we needed a different; a revolutionary and primal model of church.

The story of the great commission is not a parable, rather it describes the moment the community that had formed around the great Storyteller was propelled to become a movement of love-communities that would explode all over the world.

They were to be communities of men and women, boys and girls who *knew* what had happened to them; who *knew* what had happened to the human race. These communities were to be patterns for how the world was to be.

This knowledge was their light. Ignorance of it was darkness and blindness. Their communities would be the light of the world. That knowledge was all they needed to live out of love, for the knowledge told them that love had become their new nature.

That knowledge told them that they had been present in the vicarious death, resurrection and ascension of Jesus. The great Storyteller was also the great Storymaker!

That's why they baptised - they re-enacted the story in water.

Easy

Jesus had said, "keep bringing people from all over the world into what we've had"

The eleven responded, "That'll be easy, who wouldn't want a life of fellowship with the happy God … and with us!"

And they were right. It would only be a matter of days when one hundred and twenty happy followers of the Master became three thousand - and that was just the first day!

Soon there were another five thousand.
After that it was simply multitudes.
And before the early church's letter writers had finished – ten thousand times ten thousand and thousands of thousands!

Who wouldn't want the love, the laughter, the purpose, the freedom, the wonder of koinonia in the family on earth, fully reflecting the awesomeness of the family in heaven?

Koinonia? Oh, that's a Greek word found in the New Testament to describe the rich enjoyment of doing life together, sharing encouragement, affection and ideas with one another; living life in the happy fellowship and mutual purpose of community. It's the word that best describes the family in heaven – the community of Three – the loving Father, his Son, Jesus and the wonderful person we know as the Holy Spirit.

The communities of those who *knew* what had happened to them would be reflections of that community of Three.

Make disciples ... God-learners

Everyone had stopped learning, instead of learning they were waiting:

They were all born into a land under foreign occupation. The Romans had been there for almost a century. Familiarity and resignation was the national mood.

Their theology, their religion was settled – or so they were told. The Temple priests had it all figured out and dished out rules and requirements that stifled curiosity and all eagerness to learn something new.

Asking questions was, well, out of the question.
They were a nation of waiters, not learners.
Sound familiar?

... people who have transitioned themselves from learners with voracious appetites for truth ... to people now just waiting for the next big thing?

From people with an insatiable God-curiosity ... now just waiting for that revival, or the next anointed man or woman of God to show up?

When Jesus said, go and make disciples, at its most simple level, he was saying "go and turn people from being waiters to learners; from being resigned to monotonous familiarity, to people with an avid God-curiosity; people who just want to learn."

If this is true, we should be disciples all our lives – we never graduate; there is no certificate of completion!

As soon as you've got it all figured out: there's no longer an unfinished God-book on your bedside table; the appetite to discover something fresh and new is no longer gnawing at you – this was never the life Jesus envisioned for us!

Teach them love

The eleven were commissioned to teach the God-learners "to obey everything I have commanded you."

So we ought to see what Jesus' commandments were. We know the ten commandments and we know that the Old Covenant was riddled with commands and observances - but what about Jesus, what were his commands to the God-learners?

> "Love the Lord your God with all your heart and with all your soul and with all your mind. This is the greatest and first commandment. And the second is like it: Love your neighbour as yourself. All the Law and the Prophets hang on these two commandments." (Matthew 22:36-40)

"I give you a new commandment, that you love one another. Just as I have loved you." (John 13:34-35)

"I am giving you these commands so that you may love one other." (John 15:9-17)

The World

The Roman Empire was at that time enjoying the Pax Romana (Roman peace) which Emperor Augustus established from Spain to the Black Sea, from Egypt to the English Channel.

There are between 70 and 100 million people living in the Roman Empire and half are slaves - the personal property of their masters.

Few in the Roman Empire are part of the wealthy senatorial class. Most belong to the poor plebeian class. More than half the population is dependent on the regular distribution of free grain.

This is the scene all over the empire, including Jerusalem.

There are between three and eight million Jews in the Empire. And because the Jews had strange beliefs and strange practices (keeping the Sabbath, not eating pork, circumcision), they are despised by most Greeks and Romans.

And the Jews themselves were hardly excited about their religion, they were slaves to stifling regulations and requirements with no fresh touch from heaven in sight.

Here they all are. Partiality, suspicion, intolerance, a victim-mentality, pride, resentment, envy and for vast numbers, a resignation that they would die as unfulfilled and as unhappy as they lived.

And Jesus says, go and make disciples, teaching them to love God, to love their fellow man, to love themselves and to love all the other God-learners.

Create a love community among ...

the rich and poor,
the victors and the victims,
the Jews and Greeks,
male and females,
the haves and have nots,
the senators and the plebs,
the slaves and the free,
the prideful and the resentful.

... bring them together as a people who want to learn love.

I think that's near impossible, except for this: they were not being commissioned to reconcile people to God and to one another. They were being commissioned to announce that the world - every one - had already been reconciled, forgiven, accepted, adopted, brought to death and raised to life as one united humanity in Christ.

Their message was news ... astonishing good news!

They were bringing light to darkness. Knowledge to ignorance. Repentance to excluding mindsets. Faith to unbelief. Sight to the blind.

This was the story of stories. This was the story of the great Storyteller and the whole world caught up in him!

Can we press the reset button for church? Please?

<u>Matthew 28:18-20</u>

I've not lost anything, in fact, I'm holding everything, I have all the keys! Heaven and earth, the world and the underworld - all the keys!

Keep bringing people from all over the world into what we've had: the love, the laughter, the freedom, the community of purpose and power, fellowship with the happy God.

Go and turn people from being waiters to learners; from being resigned to monotonous familiarity, to people with a voracious God-curiosity, people who just want to learn.

When they know what's happened - that the new creation has come - they'll want to celebrate. Baptise them!

Teach them love. To love God, to love their fellow man, to love themselves and to love all the other God-learners.

And it'll be as presence-filled for them as it was around the shores of Galilee with me - without interruption - forever!

(The Great Commission - Jesus)

Selah
Pause | Consider | Apply

During a reading of Psalms (songs) the word Selah is included in the text to ask the singer to pause - a brief interlude to ponder the composition is being called for. Following each chapter of The Storyteller, you will find an invitation to "pause, consider and apply" - to personalise what you have just read by completing three intentionally open sentences. Alternatively, the Selah interlude can be used to trigger discussion and testimony in a group.

The Great Commission

If I place myself on the mountain with the eleven, my emotions are …

To be a God-learner, I have decided to …

I would describe my relationship with the Church as …

Chapter Thirteen
The Pearl of Great Value

Matthew 13:45-46

The merchant's jaw dropped. He'd not seen anything like it - ever! A pearl of such extraordinary beauty.

He was at first struck by its colour and sheen. It was a rare white pearl with rose coloured overtones; its lustre was not a surface shine, it was an intense brightness that illuminated from within - the light being reflected throughout its various layers.

This was an experienced vendor of precious gems who would journey long distances to find the specimens he was looking for. He knew that the mollusc had coated a grain of sand that had slipped inside with layer after layer of nacre until the gleaming prize was formed.

The deep iridescence the merchant observed told him the little shellfish had suffered much with the grating intruder for many layers of nacre had been produced to coat the irritant. The nacre thickness and quality would mean this pearl would be virtually timeless and the light that would be reflected through its layers would be of unmatched beauty and appeal.

He had to have it. It felt as if it was everything he'd ever been searching for and now he'd found it. No price was too much to pay and so he sold all he had and bought it.

A large crowd had been listening to the Storyteller as he sat just offshore in his friend's boat. The crowd had stood on the beach and from the very first story he told - the one about the sower - no one wanted to go home. They were hearing about generosity, about grace and about joy. They were more than pensive as he mentioned a sinister plot to ruin his mission - the weeds among the wheat.

However, their countenance changed when hearing the stories of mustard seed and yeast. What an extraordinary kingdom this King was speaking of ... what a glorious future awaited the world!

They would be pondering the story of the hidden treasure for a long time to come but as soon as he started talking about the pearl it felt like an invitation to everyone of them and somehow they knew that, like the merchant, they had found the "pearl" in this Storyteller and the stories he told.

They knew this "pearl" of goodness, peace and joy had strongly confronted the Jewish legalists ... and they had grated against it. However, the Storyteller's stories were patently clear to them, the "pearl of immense value" would become ever more radiant with every opposition it would suffer.

As they stood there on the beach ... listening ... every man, woman, boy and girl knew they had found a kingdom and a King for whom no price was too high to follow.

Could we with ink the ocean fill,
And were the skies of parchment made,
Were every stalk on earth a quill,
And every man a scribe by trade;
To write the love of God above
Would drain the ocean dry;
Nor could the scroll contain the whole,
Though stretched from sky to sky.

(Frederick Lehman, 1917 hymn writer: The Love of God)

I don't know which of the characters describe me best: the journeying merchant or someone from the crowd on the beach? Needless to say, in 2009 I found the pearl. I had encountered the King of love and what I saw and felt and learned was more precious than all the other pearls. It was the very thing for which my soul had longed: a vision, a relationship, a knowledge of such beauty and grandeur no price was too high to have it.

As the weeks and months unfolded it was as if the pearl's structure was reflecting layer after layer for me to see. And the things I was seeing started seeping out of me as I led and shared in ministry at Elevate.

Amy

One Sunday morning Amy spoke with me; she had been attending the services with her boyfriend for several weeks. Up until then, Amy had had little exposure to the Christian Church or its message; a delightful young woman, typical of her generation.

Amy had been hearing the word "grace" at Elevate ... a lot. Love, forgiveness and unconditional, were words that would have joined "grace" on the frequently heard list. I was a storyteller and my story was becoming more generous, more kind.

It seemed so simple, so understated but Amy wanted me to know that she believed the grace, she believed the love. Amy knew that God was for her; now she was for God.

It meant a lot to me. I had long abandoned a methodology that brought people to faith with underlying threats of hell and emotional, urgent appeals. I wanted to believe that if someone saw the pearl, they would choose it. Amy was the first person who convinced me they would.

I was reminded of St John's confession, "So we have known and believe the love that God has for us." (1 John 4:16). John had called himself "the one whom Jesus loved" when writing his Gospel (John 13:23) ... it's not that he thought he was alone in being loved by Jesus, it's just that he felt like the most loved person in the entire world! He'd found the pearl.

Lament

As a young pastor, I was an associate of a national ministry movement that held conferences for their members annually, sometimes more often. I was always in awe when listening to my seniors unpack scripture after scripture as they presented teaching and revelation that had been thrilling them and their church.

Sometimes the speakers were from overseas and the approach didn't seem to change … they were sharing their pearls.

A decade later a significant shift was underway. The Church Growth movement was taking off and with it a new set of words became part of the lexicon at our conferences. Leadership, vision, strategy, technique, goals, excellence, team, program … and the list went on.

Taking a back seat were the words that once energised and amazed us: kingdom, cross, grace, bride, presence, love, relationship …

Too few lamented the change. The enticement of success, corporate style, had replaced the jaw dropping experience of the journeying merchant.

A World Wide Web

Those were the days when most Christian's "spiritual food" came through the pulpit of their local church: the pastor had considerable control over what was being taught and who was invited to speak. If the pastor's "food" was changing, if the pearl was being locked away for safe keeping, the flock in turn were hearing less and less of what once awed them.

No one saw it coming but Computer scientists Vinton Cerf and Bob Kahn invented the internet. By the early 1990's the World Wide Web was spreading into homes all over the world … social media by the early 2000's. The pastors and their pulpits no longer had a monopoly on the message. If Christian books had been troublesome, they were the gently lapping wave compared to the tsunami of online spiritual opinion, blogs, videos, theology, history and so on.

I had become an avid reader of Trinitarian theology and of authors who conveyed a more generous inclusion, a deeper appreciation for mystery and the primacy of love. I started connecting with podcasts and found most of my new favourite authors on social media. The books I was reading and the internet became bountiful sources for … nacre … for the iridescent layers that provide layer after layer of depth and beauty to the pearl.

Through the internet I found a large and growing community of lovers and learners … pearl hunters. Among them, an ever growing company of friends who live in these islands of New Zealand.

The Mixed Bag

The Edict of Milan (313 AD) brought about a massive shift. The Christ movement became the religion of Rome. Persecution would cease, favour would be granted, basilicas would be built, the Church's leaders would be granted status.

But because Rome was a military Empire of conquest and enrichment, the Church would have to 'revise' its moral opposition to violence and the accumulation of wealth, to slavery and nepotism. A new morality was adopted, focussing upon matters of individual sexuality. Simple living, affection for all, nonviolence and love of enemies, all but lost their voice.

Relationship - the shape of God as Trinity - was no longer as important. The Father became angry and distant, Jesus was reduced to a facilitator of God appeasement, the Holy Spirit was forgotten.

Churches were gifted prime city sites for their magnificent houses of worship. Christianity moved from infiltrating society as a missional movement, to one that would defend its status and attract its adherents by multiple means and media.

From that time on it was a mixed bag. Other pearls had become popular that were dubious imitations of what the early Church fathers and mothers had held dear. Doctrinal theories concerning hell, the atonement and predestination arose. Theology known as futurism and dispensationalism became mainstream.

The Early Church Fathers and Mothers

Practically all of the faith-basics Suzanne and I were raised with were formed after the Edict of Milan. However, now we were learning from the great hearts and minds from the earliest days of the faith; the first three hundred years of the Christ movement, some of whom had been discipled by the Biblical Apostles. We were learning truths close to their uncontaminated source.

a more generous inclusion:

"All men are Christ's, some by knowing him, the rest not yet. He is the Saviour, not of some but of all. For how is he Saviour and Lord, if not the Saviour and Lord of all he created in his very image?" Clement of Alexandria (150-215 AD) a deeper appreciation for mystery:

"Jesus Christ, in his infinite love, has become what we are, in order that he may make us entirely what he is." Irenaeus of Lyon (130-202 AD)

the primacy of love:

"Among us, you will find uneducated persons, and artisans, and old women, who, even if they cannot prove the benefit of [our faith] through words, through their deeds they prove the benefit that results from our devotion; for they do not memorize speeches, but rather they exhibit good works; when struck, they do not strike back, and when they are robbed, they do not bring charges; to everyone who asks of them, they give, and they love their neighbours as themselves." Athenagoras of Athens (133-190 AD).

Coinciding with retirement, Suzanne and I formed a Book Club … precious friends who had found the pearl joined in. Some favourite authors visited our shores and we banded together to meet them, to receive from them and strengthen our links with pilgrim brothers and sisters around the globe. What a rich thing it is to know you're not walking alone with your pearl.

We have felt cheered on by friends the world over and by merchants from all across history. Our jaws have not stopped dropping at what we've found. We know, we're convinced, this pearl will continue to reveal its depth, it's layers and its iridescent beauty … endlessly.

Selah
Pause | Consider | Apply

During a reading of Psalms (songs) the word Selah is included in the text to ask the singer to pause - a brief interlude to ponder the composition is being called for. Following each chapter of The Storyteller, you will find an invitation to "pause, consider and apply" - to personalise what you have just read by completing three intentionally open sentences. Alternatively, the Selah interlude can be used to trigger discussion and testimony in a group.

The Pearl of Great Value

My jaw dropped when …

I do have a lament concerning the Church, it's …

I'm not walking alone with my pearl, I have …

Epilogue

By now you'll realise that this has been a very personal project for me; a celebration of things that have touched and changed me deeply.

I chose a retelling of the parables of Jesus as a vehicle to share my experience, my shifts in understanding, my widened vision and my bigger hopes for the Church and the world.

If I was a theologian, I might have chosen a far more analytical and detailed approach. I would not have traced a history from my great, great grand-parents, highlighted all my important moments and told the story of my and Suzanne's life together in family and in vocation.

I love theology but I'm more comfortable as a storyteller, that's why I've readily drawn upon the talents of people like Baxter Kruger, Ben Myers, François DuToit, Dietrich Bonhoeffer, C.S. Lewis and Karl Barth.

Am I annunciating their theology? No, I'd be sure to irritate each of them if I tried. They're simply helping me, with a few inspiring and affirming quotes, tell my story. Nevertheless, I have read these scholars far more widely than these quotes may indicate; each of these men have helped me chart another crossing on the journey.

It could be that my story and my retelling of these parables has resonated with your own journey and affirmed your own God-picture. I hope I have cheered you on and emboldened you in your spiritual adventure.

Alternatively, you just can't get your head around some, maybe most of what I'm conveying. You may be ready to argue a few points with me. We live in a diverse, colourful world - it's God's world - and it seems that's also true about worldviews, God-pictures and interpretations of inspired scripture.

So thank you for reading this work by someone who finds himself in a different interpretive corner. I sincerely pray that you are as enthralled by your own journey, as I am with mine. The world needs enthralled people; there are men and women enough who have lost the thrill of compelling curiosity and transcendent discovery. We may be different but let's both be enthralled.

Biblical scholar, Peter Enns, titled a recent book "The Sin of Certainty". It's an appeal to respect the Christian scriptures enough to realise they aren't as certain or unified about nearly as many things as we would like them to be. In fact, they don't give us permission to possess a cut and dried belief system that shuts the door on a life of searching with questions, digging deeper, listening broadly and conversing graciously.

What the Scriptures do call us to is an awestruck belief in the reality of the benevolent Divine who is fully revealed in the person of Jesus Christ: who lived among ordinary people as their Saviour, indeed the Saviour of the world. The Scriptures call us to dynamic love and relationship with the Family in heaven and on earth. It's in the lively grip of relationship that the most liberating and satisfying theology emerges.

I have a fond memory of sitting at lunch with Bible expositor Derek Prince. I was young and hopeful of being a pastor one day. Dr Prince shared many things, but only one I still remember fifty years later: "Revelation comes out of fellowship," this wise man said.

In my story, you will have realised that I've been certain more than once about my closed interpretive conclusions, only to have encountered the Living Word and have my theological apple cart tipped over. To strain the metaphor, I never did retrieve all the spilled apples but I found other varieties of fruit, placed them in the cart and went on my way again. I now push my theological cart with much less certainty than I once did (ever curious and always hopeful).

I've been asked if I am a universalist. I can understand why I'm asked that - it's the things I say about

... the world being reconciled to God in Christ;
... God's universal love for humanity and their inclusion in the
     death, resurrection and ascension of Christ;
... my dismissal of an eternal conscious torment model of hell
... that love keeps no record of wrongs, never gives up and that
     God is love;
... and my hint at the possibility of post-mortem response to love.

I suspect there's a secret universalist in a lot of people - especially those with a deceased loved one, someone they deeply loved who was only ever good to them but didn't seem to comply with the prescription for entry to heaven. I mean, wouldn't it be marvellous to be wrong about that!

Imagine, you've "been there ten thousand years bright shining as the sun" and you summon up the courage to ask Jesus if your loved one has been punished enough for not believing in him - surely after ten thousand years of being kept alive in conscious torment the punishment has fit the crime?

If not a secret universalist, maybe a secret *hopeful* universalist.

There is a span of seven generations to my grandchildren from William and Elizabeth Purdie who migrated under billowing sails and reached these shores on Christmas Day 1849. It was a journey of hope, courage, loss and of new adventure. Their journey has provided a metaphor for the pilgrimage that has taken me to a new land of wonder and discovery.

The metaphor of migration was brilliantly used by Brian McLaren in his 2016 book "The Great Spiritual Migration". Brian writes, "The Christian story, from Genesis until now, is fundamentally about people on the move". Of our time he observes, "Growing numbers of Christians are moving away from defining themselves by lists of beliefs and towards a way of life defined by love." Brian's invitation to us is to set out on "the most significant spiritual pilgrimage of our time: to help Christianity become more Christian."

As much as anything, I want to encourage you to be a God-learner, to be that "one who Jesus loved" in a community of other God-learners, pilgrims and merchant travellers. I want to encourage you to always have an unfinished book on the side-table next to your favourite chair. In case it's helpful, following this Epilogue is a bibliography and in it you'll find a catalogue of books that have spurred me forward and excited my heart page after page.

Last of all; find that thing you are truly passionate about - anything! That thing that fills you up with light, that when contemplating it … it makes you the happiest person on earth. It's the thing that enthrals you, that 'gathers a crowd on the beach', that makes a storyteller out of you.

Bibliography

The following books have either been referenced or quoted in The Storyteller's text, or have inspired the telling of my story.

Chapter One

The Shack: Where Tragedy Confronts Eternity
    by Wm. Paul Young (Windblown Media 2007)
God is for Us by C. Baxter Kruger (Perichoresis Press 2008)
The Divine Dance by Richard Rohr (SPCK Publishing 2016)
Water to Wine: Some of My Story by Brian Zahnd
    (Spello Press 2016)

Chapter Two

The Mystery of Christ & why we don't get it by Robert Farrar
    Capon (Wm. B. Eerdmans-Lightning Source 1993)
The Hyper-grace Gospel by Paul Ellis (KingsPress 2014)
Raptureless: An Optimistic Guide to the End of the World
    (Third Edition) by Jonathan Welton © 2012

Chapter Three

Heavy Rain by Kris Vallotton (Regal Books 2010)
The Showings of Julian of Norwich by Mirabai Starr
    (Hampton Roads Publishing 2013)
The Art of Revelation by Jonathan Welton © 2017
What We Talk About When we Talk About God by Rob Bell
    (HarperOne 2014)

Chapter Four

Simply Good News by N.T. Wright (HarperOne 2017)
Letters and Papers from Prison by Dietrich Bonhoeffer
    (Touchstone 1997)
Kingdom Grace Judgment by Robert Farrar Capon
    (William B. Eerdmans Publishing Co 2002)

Chapter Five

The Apostles' Creed by Benjamin Myers (Lexham Press 2018)

Crux, Mors, Inferi: A Primer and Reader on Christ's Descent
by Samuel Renihan (© 2021 Samuel D Renihan)

Chapter Six

The Three Apologies of G.K. Chesterton: Heretics, Orthodoxy
& The Everlasting Man by G.K. Chesterton
(Mockingbird Press 2018)

Jesus and the Undoing of Adam by C. Baxter Kruger
(Perichoresis Press 2011)

Karl Barth in Plain English by Stephen D. Morrison
(Beloved Publishing 2017)

Intermission

Love is the Way: Holding on to Hope in Troubling Times by
Michael Curry and Sara Grace (Avery September 22, 2020)

Eager to Love: The Alternative Way of Francis of Assisi
by Richard Rohr (Franciscan Media 2016)

When Breath becomes Air: What makes life worth living in the
face of death by Paul Kalanithi (Vintage / Penguin Random
House 2016)

Chapter Seven

The Youngest Day: Shelter Island's Seasons in the Light of
Grace by Robert Farrar Capon (Mockingbird Ministries 2019)

Karl Barth: His Life from Letters and Autobiographical Texts
by Eberhard Busch (Philadelphia: Fortress, 1976)

The Furious Longing of God by Brennan Manning
(David C Cook 2009)

Chapter Eight

The Brothers Karamazov by Fyodor Dostoevsky
(Penguin Classics 1982)

Sinners in the Hands of a Loving God by Brian Zahnd
(WaterBrook 2017)

Jesus Undefeated: Condemning the False Doctrine of Eternal
Torment by Keith Giles (Quoir 2019)

Chapter Nine

The Shack Revisited by C. Baxter Kruger (FaithWords 2012)

Conjectures of a Guilty Bystander by Thomas Merton
(Image; Reissue edition1968)

Lost Connections: Uncovering the real causes of depression -
and the unexpected solutions by Johann Hari
(Bloomsbury 2018)

Chapter Ten

A More Christlike God: A More Beautiful Gospel
by Bradley Jersak (Plain Truth Ministries 2016)

Lies We Believe About God by Wm. Paul Young
(Atria Books; Reprint edition 2018)

What's Wrong with the World by G.K. Chesterton
(Dover Publications 2007)

Chapter Eleven

The Chronicles of Narnia - The Last Battle by C.S. Lewis
(HarperCollins; Illustrated edition 2002)

Mirror Study Bible by François DuToit's
(Mirrorword Publishing; Revised edition 2018)

Into the Abyss: Discover Your True Identity in the Infinite Depths of
Christ by Mo Thomas (Eyes Open Pres 2020)

Chapter Twelve

The Untold Story of the New Testament Church by Frank Viola
(Destiny Image 2005)

The Shaping of Things To Come by Michael Frost and Alan
Hirsch (Baker Books 2013)

Searching for Sunday: Loving, Leaving and Finding the Church
by Rachel Held Evans (Thomas Nelson 2015)

Chapter Thirteen

A More Christlike Word: Reading Scripture the Emmaus Way
by Bradley Jersak (Whitaker House 2021)

The Ragamuffin Gospel: Good News for the Bedraggled, Beat-
Up, and Burnt Out by Brennan Manning (Multnomah 2005)

Dancing Standing Still: Healing the World from a Place of
Prayer by Richard Rohr (Paulist Press: 2014)

Cosmos Reborn : Happy Theology on the New Creation
by John Crowder (Sons of Thunder 2013)

Epilogue

The Sin of Certainty: Why God Desires Our Trust More Than
Our "Correct" Beliefs by Peter Enns (HarperOne 2017)

Love Wins: A Book About Heaven, Hell, and the Fate of Every
Person Who Ever Lived by Rob Bell (HarperOne 2012)

The Great Dance: The Christian Vision Revisited
by C. Baxter Kruger (Perichoresis Press 2011)

The Great Spiritual Migration by Brian McLaren
(Hodder & Stoughton 2016)

Glossary

Abba
>'Father' - also used as the term of tender endearment by a beloved child, i.e. daddy; papa.

Age of accountability
>considered by some Christian teachers to be the age a young person must reach before being punishable for their own sins.

Apocalyptic
>momentous or catastrophic - world-ending.

Ascension
>the phenomena of Jesus Christ's re-entry into the heavens following his earthly life, death, burial and resurrection.

Atonement
>to make one, to reconcile. In Theology there are a range of theories of how atonement was achieved between a holy God and a fallen humanity. To be Christian, an atonement theory places Jesus Christ at its centre as mankind's atonement.

Baptise (Baptism)
>symbolic re-enactment of death, burial and resurrection in water. Celebration of the New Covenant.

Calling
>a call to service, a spiritual vocation.

Commission

>a mission, role or project given from a higher authority to a person or group that carries the necessary authority to carry it out.

Cosmic

>world-wide.

Covenant

>in the Bible - the basis for relationship, acceptance and participation with God. Jesus Christ ushered in a new covenant for the whole world.

Discipline

>practices of a particular craft, task or philosophy - in Christianity, disciplines are practices like prayer, study, silence, worship, solitude, etc.

Dispensationalism

>an interpretive system that divides history into separate eras in which God's plan is administered. It includes a concept of restored Jewish nationalism in the End Time.

Dualistic

>thinking that makes a distinction between what is perceived to be good and what is regarded as evil.

Eternal Conscious Torment (ECT)

>a teaching of the afterlife concerning hell as a place where God keeps the unrepentant alive and conscious, eternally suffering torment and fiery torture, without any possibility of escape. ECT was first articulated by Augustine in 410 AD.

Eucharist

observing Christ's last supper when he broke bread and served wine and related it to his body and blood that would be broken and shed on the cross. The communion service. The celebration of the New Covenant.

Franciscan

of the Order of St Francis of Assisi.

Futurism

an apocalyptic interpretation of many major portions of the Bible as future, e.g. the Book of Daniel, Matthew 24, the Book of Revelation.

Godhead

a term to denote the Trinity - Father, Son and Holy Spirit - the three person's of God who reveal the true one God.

Gospel

Good news. The story of mankind's salvation and ascension through Jesus Christ.

Grace

the gift of God's favourable endowment bestowed rather than earned or merited, which carries with it the power to "be".

Hyper-Calvinism

(also called 6-point Calvinism, or Double Predestination). Belief that God chooses some for salvation and some for perdition (eternal torment) and that He does so not on the basis that some people are better or worse than others, but simply through His sovereign choice.

Indigenous

originating or occurring naturally in a particular place; native. E.g. the first peoples of a country.

Judaizers

Jewish zealots from the time of the early church who opposed the New Covenant and the young Church, seeking to force them to adopt the rituals and requirements of the Temple with their faith in Christ, or to abandon Christ altogether.

Kingdom

a realm of rulership, where a king reigns - in the Bible the Kingdom of God or the Kingdom of heaven are the same, these terms speak of life and society overseen by God's goodness, peace and joy.

Kiwi

a native bird of New Zealand, used symbolically to denote New Zealand people.

Last Days

the period between the birth of Jesus to the destruction of the temple in Jerusalem in 70A D. Essentially the last days of the Old Covenant.

Māori

the indigenous people of New Zealand.

Messiah

the promised deliverer of the Jewish nation prophesied in the Hebrew Bible. Jesus, regarded by Christians as the Messiah of the Hebrew prophecies and the Saviour of humankind.

Ministries

> departments or areas of service.

Missionary

> a person being sent to another place to share the good news about Jesus Christ.

Most Holy Place

> the inner sanctuary of the Jewish Temple where God was present in the days before the Golden Ark was missing. Also the Holy of Holies. Heaven on earth.

Mystic

> a person who is familiar with inner experiences of God.

Olivet Discourse

> a suite of predictions, warnings, prophecies and parables from Jesus Christ in response to questions from his disciples about when the Temple in Jerusalem would be destroyed and what the end of the Temple age would be like. Found in the first three Gospels. Fulfilled in AD 70.

Orthodoxy

> the Church and its accepted beliefs, especially from the close of Biblical history through the first millennium AD. A large part of the Christian Church today other than Roman Catholic or Protestant, e.g. Greek Orthodox, Russian Orthodox, Eastern Orthodox, etc.

Othering

> the phenomenon in which an individual or group is defined and labelled as not fitting within one's own "normal" or "approved". They are "other".

Pastor

>a Christian minister who leads and cares for the people in a church.

Pharisees

>a sect of Jewish priests, politicians and businessmen who arose around 100 years before Christ and opposed Christ during his ministry.

Predestination

>the doctrine that God has ordained all that will happen, especially with regard to the salvation of some and not others.

Repent

>to think differently, to have another (a change of) mind.

Retribution

>punishment inflicted on someone as vengeance for a wrong or criminal act.

Sabbatical

>a period of time set aside from ones usual occupation to refresh and study. Literally "seventh", i.e. one year in every seven.

Scribes

>a professional group of record keepers in Israel during the time of Christ. As those who copied laws and Jewish history, they opposed Christ on legalistic grounds from the Jewish scriptures.

Sheol

> a place of the departed, the grave - a Hebrew word found in the Old Testament of the Bible.

Synagogue

> Jewish places of worship that were established during the centuries between the Old and New Testaments, when the Jewish nation was in captivity or had no Temple.

Theologian

> a person who is engaged in the study of God and God things (Greek: Theo = God, logy = study)

Tongues

> languages - in the Bible an unusual ability to speak languages previously unlearnt, but inspired by the Holy Spirit. (See Acts Chapter 2.)

Torah

> The Jewish name for the first five books of the Bible that contained the story of the birth of their nation and the law of requirements associated with Moses and the Old Covenant.

Trinitarian Theology

> belief that emphasises the relational / love essence of God and the work of Christ in representing all mankind in his death, resurrection and ascension, thus including them in his own relationship within the Trinity. (Notable Trinitarian theologians: C.S. Lewis, T.F. Torrance, Karl Barth, C. Baxter Kruger.)

Trinity

    the "community" of God in three persons - the Father, the Son and the Holy Spirit.

Universalism

    (Christian Universalist)

    a belief that all humanity is eternally saved because of God's all-including reconciling work on the cross of Christ that reveals his self-giving, radically forgiving and relentless love for all.

    (Hopeful Universalist - Christian)

    a hope that not one member of the human race will forever refuse the self-giving, radically forgiving and relentless love of God.

Vicariously (Vicarious)

    on behalf of another so that the experience and its consequences are as true for them as for the primary person. Humanity's inclusion in Christ's life, death, resurrection and ascension was vicarious.

Visitation

    a Biblical term meaning a "coming" of God to intervene for their good and blessing.

By the same Author:

The Latter Rain Revival
The New Zealand Story

Fifty years ago I started hearing of a unique spiritual revival in 1948, Saskatchewan, Canada, and the impact that flowed all the way to Australia and New Zealand. For thirty four years I was mentored and ministered in the experiences and teaching of the Latter Rain Revival.

In this book you'll meet the men who pioneered the 1948 outpouring in New Zealand. How did it start and spread? How important was it? Is "Latter Rain" still with us today? What lessons can we learn? This is the New Zealand story.

David Collins

Available on Kindle or from Amazon and Book Depository

Lightning Source UK Ltd.
Milton Keynes UK
UKHW011600091121
393673UK00003B/835